"Sometimes we get closer to truth by taking the [illegible] we typically take. *Empathy for the Devil* gets us closer to truth by exploring the dark side, the devil's side. Like a series of narrative proverbs, we can learn something about what is right by looking closely at what is wrong."

Thomas Jay Oord, author of *The Uncontrolling Love of God*

"This is a beautifully written, compelling, and important book that will make you see the villains of the Bible and yourself in a whole new light. Highly recommended."

Matt Mikalatos, author of *Sky Lantern*

"*Empathy for the Devil* is unlike anything you've ever read. Part fictional anthology, part nonfiction, the pages of this book bring ancient antagonists to life in ways that will both shock and inform you. It's *Wicked* for the spiritual formation set. Every one of us knows what it's like to linger before a mirror, seeing a deep secret or two we withhold from the world, wondering if others really understand our hearts, anxious about whether or not we want them to. When JR. told me he was going to write a book about how relatable the villains of Scripture are, I thought if anyone could pull it off, he could. And he has. The people in these pages are infamous for the worst things they ever thought and did. Plenty of us can probably relate to the fear of being remembered for our faults, what we got wrong. But beyond the darkness there is always a light to move toward. This book shows us the cost of selfish ambition and the choice we have to be protagonists in a story much larger than ourselves."

Clay Morgan, author of *Undead: Revived, Resuscitated & Reborn*

"The deepest truth usually dawns on us through the power of a story. Nowhere do we find more explosiveness than in the stories of Scripture. We love these stories because they're not whitewashed or edited. We see ourselves in our human rawness. JR. Forasteros has done two things quite well in this book: narrated the story of the dark characters of Scripture and introduced them into our lives in believable terms. If we can own them rather than castigate them, we may find the saving grace of God that delivers us from evil."

Dan Boone, president, Trevecca Nazarene University, Nashville

"We underestimate the power of looking to our greatest enemies. We forget that they are like us more than they are unlike us and that if we can learn to see ourselves in their eyes, to bridge the gap between 'us' and 'them,' tremendous healing and peace can be found. Never has there been a time in history where this message is more needed, and JR. tackles the subject with creativity, wisdom, and grace. You don't want to miss this book."

Allison Fallon, author of *Packing Light*

"Reading *Empathy for the Devil* is like realizing your whole life you've been trying to see the stars through the wrong end of the telescope. Carefully researched and creatively written, *Empathy for the Devil* gives us a new kind of Copernican Revolution. It reframes the way we think about the other and the Other. I feel like I can see the stars with fresh eyes—or maybe for the first time."

Tom Fuerst, author of *Underdogs and Outsiders*

"The most compelling question any great story seeks to answer is *why?* Why did Cain kill Abel? Why did Delilah seduce Samson? Why did Judas betray Jesus? These questions are all the same question: Why does evil exist? And, more to the point, why does it exist within us? In *Empathy for the Devil,* JR. Forasteros tells seven gripping stories about the most infamous characters of the Bible so we can learn why they did what they did, and, in turn, why we do what we do. Tread lightly, reader: when JR. parts the veil over Jezebel's face or grants us entrance into Herod's inner sanctum, you're unlikely to discover the evil adversaries you booed in Sunday school. Rather, you're going to find yourself subtly nodding your head. You will see these misunderstood men and women of the Bible in such arresting, startling new ways that you may even catch glimpses of yourself in their eyes. The question you have to ask yourself then is *why?*"

Blake Atwood, author of *The Gospel According to Breaking Bad*

"It's easy to pass over the villains of the Bible, dismissing them as foils of the story, convinced that they're not like us. But JR. Forasteros says, 'Not so fast!' Even though we rightly admire the heroes of the Bible, JR. holds up the mirror of Scripture and invites us to ask, *Mirror, mirror, on the wall, who's the vilest of them all?* It's not who you think. *Empathy for the Devil* is a creative, insightful, provocative look at the villains of the Bible, not just as cautionary tales but also as exemplars of the human condition—our common lot. Here is wisdom: by identifying with these 'bad boys and girls' (*Oh, my villainous heart!*), JR. helps us see how we can become incarnational models of God's redemption in Christ."

Rodney Reeves, dean, Redford Professor of Biblical Studies,
Southwest Baptist University

"A tendency of triumphalist Christianity and American exceptionalism, and really just human pride, is that it tends more and more toward ignoring its own weaknesses and sin. *Empathy for the Devil* helps curb this tendency by exploring the shapes and contours, the colors and smells, of our faults. These expanded and gentler retellings of biblical villains' stories create much-needed space for our own brokenness and for God's grace to transform, not just triumph over, the devil in all of us."

Tim Basselin, associate professor of media, arts, and worship,
Dallas Theological Seminary

"*Empathy for the Devil* is as provocative a read as it is informative to the very way Christians respond to both the sinfulness within our own human hearts and the world all around. This is a must-read for those with any interest in loving the downtrodden, mistaken, failures, and misfits often all too quickly marginalized and remembered only by their shortcomings."

Guy Delcambre, author of *Earth and Sky*

"Researchers have demonstrated a correlation between reading fiction and a capacity for empathy. This should not surprise us, for both require attentiveness, imagination, and the ability to enter into another's story. Synthesizing solid yet accessible biblical scholarship, fictionalized retellings of biblical narratives, and pastoral wisdom, JR. Forasteros invites us to consider the perspectives of familiar and not-so-familiar villains of the Bible. *Empathy for the Devil* performs a kind of 'listening between the lines' for the desires, motivations, and rationalizations of even the most despicable characters and their (mis)deeds. The point is not to elevate them, but to humble us. Their stories, carefully considered, expose similar tendencies and twistedness lurking within our own hearts. Every reader will benefit not only from JR.'s insights into these cautionary tales, but from the exercise of entering empathetically into their stories and allowing the Holy Spirit to shine the flashlight into the darkest corners of our souls."

Brannon Hancock, associate professor of practical theology and worship, Wesley Seminary at Indiana Wesleyan University

"Identifying society's villains may be the amusement of our day. We rally outrage (usually via social media) and direct it toward our enemies, distancing ourselves from their errors and evils. In *Empathy for the Devil*, JR. Forasteros beckons us to reconsider our judgments. With beautiful prose and solid biblical exposition, Forasteros kneads empathy into readers' hearts as we see our common need of rescue from evil—a rescue God graciously provides in Christ Jesus to villains like you and me."

Erin Straza, author of *Comfort Detox* and managing editor at *Christ and Pop Culture*

"Written with the biblical knowledge of a scholar, the incisive wisdom of a prophet, and an imagination worthy of the Inklings, *Empathy for the Devil* expertly shines a spotlight on the 'bad guys' of the Bible so as to illumine the bad guys within our own hearts. Be ready for a page-turner that takes an inventory of your soul."

Randal Rauser, author of *What's So Confusing About Grace?*

"*Empathy for the Devil* is book that gives a fresh take on the villains of the Bible. I still remember reading the chapters on Judas and Satan for the first time. The 'frog' in my throat got bigger the more that I read it. Not only does this book give a fresh perspective, it also invites the reader to walk a mile in each villain's shoes. After walking that mile, you might ask yourself: Is there a little bit of villain in me too?"

Da MAC, recording artist

"JR. has a history of slaying giants. As a fellow 'weird pastor' I've always loved how JR. tackles the subjects all of us want to hear about but typically don't have the nerve. He mixes sharp scholastic skill with wit. He communicates not as someone who emulates popular culture but as one who truly lives and creates culture. In *Empathy for the Devil*, we get fantastic exegesis that cuts each of us right to the core. We realize evil is something truly different than what Western Christianity has created over the last few decades. I'm glad JR. wrote this book. It is one we all need to read because it teaches us about the humanity we all have. But even more than our humanity, it teaches us the power of deep, beautiful, reckless divine grace."

Chad Brooks, pastor of Foundry Church and host of The Productive Pastor podcast

"At first glance, you might be thrown off by the title. But I'd say stay with it! What Forasteros has laid out here is a popular culture ortho-theology. The era we live in is nothing less than out of the ordinary. So we need even more out-of-the-ordinary theology. This is exactly what Forasteros has done in this magnificent text. He has helped us to grasp transcendence from the margins—a theology for those who don't fit. Yes. Finally. He's given us a manifesto for our current sociocultural setting. Bravo!"

Daniel White Hodge, associate professor of intercultural communications, North Park University, author of *Homeland Insecurity* and *Hip Hop's Hostile Gospel*

"With creative genius, JR. invites us to open the floodgates to our imaginations and see things like never before. This is a thought-provoking and mind-bending book. JR. is a brilliant and articulate storyteller, and you won't be able to put this book down. So get cozy, grab a cup of coffee, and immerse yourself in this book!"

Tara Beth Leach, author of *Emboldened*

EMPATHY FOR THE DEVIL

FINDING OURSELVES IN THE VILLAINS OF THE BIBLE

JR. FORASTEROS

IVP Books
An imprint of InterVarsity Press
Downers Grove, Illinois

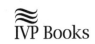

InterVarsity Press
P.O. Box 1400, Downers Grove, IL 60515-1426
ivpress.com
email@ivpress.com

InterVarsity Press® is the book-publishing division of InterVarsity Christian Fellowship/USA®, a movement of students and faculty active on campus at hundreds of universities, colleges, and schools of nursing in the United States of America, and a member movement of the International Fellowship of Evangelical Students. For information about local and regional activities, visit intervarsity.org.

Published in association with literary agent David Van Diest of the Van Diest Literary Agency, www.christianliteraryagency.com.

Author photo by Arianne Martin, www.ariannemartin.com.

Cover design: David Fassett
Interior design: Daniel van Loon
Images: devil illustration: © CSA Images / Getty Images
dark gray background: © Lava4images/iStockimages
snake illustration: David Fassett

ISBN 978-0-8308-4514-9 (print)
ISBN 978-0-8308-8896-2 (digital)

Printed in the United States of America ♾

InterVarsity Press is committed to ecological stewardship and to the conservation of natural resources in all our operations. This book was printed using sustainably sourced paper.

Library of Congress Cataloging-in-Publication Data
A catalog record for this book is available from the Library of Congress.

P 21 20 19 18 17 16 15 14 13 12 11 10 9 8 7 6 5 4 3 2 1
Y 34 33 32 31 30 29 28 27 26 25 24 23 22 21 20 19 18 17

For Amanda
(AKA Mother Terrorista).

The world is helpless
before your love's great power.
Here's what you've taught me:

CONTENTS

Introduction | 1

1 Cain | 7

2 You Wouldn't Like Me When I'm Angry:
How Anger Might Be an Invitation to Life | 19

3 Delilah and Samson | 31

4 I'm Not Like Everybody Else:
When the Light of the World Goes Dark | 47

5 Jezebel | 59

6 House of Cards:
Power, Fear, and the New American Gods | 73

7 Herod the Great | 87

8 Between Rome and a Hard Place:
Living in a World of Impossible Choices | 97

9 Herodias | 109

10 The Cat's in the Cradle:
The Fingerprints Our Families Leave on Us | 125

11 Judas | 143

12 What Death Smells Like:
The Betrayal of Faithfulness | 157

INTERLUDE: The Monster at the End of This Book | 171

13 Satan | 173

14 Running with the Devil:
On Devils, Older Brothers, and Pharisees
Then and Now | 189

EPILOGUE: Empathy for the Devil:
What to Do When It Turns Out You're the Villain | 207

Acknowledgments | 211

Notes | 217

INTRODUCTION

When I was a sophomore in high school, I wanted to challenge myself on a world history research paper. I decided to examine the worst event in the twentieth century, the Holocaust, and ask if anything good came out of it. Fortunately my history teacher, Mrs. Morgason, was wise enough to discern that I wasn't a burgeoning neo-Nazi. I was just a clueless, suburban Christian kid who didn't see the Holocaust as anything more than an event in a history book. Rather than report me to the principal or a guidance counselor, she gave my paper the poor grade it deserved and let it slip into obscurity, where it belongs.

When I graduated from high school, I went to Germany. During the trip, I visited Dachau, the site of the first Nazi concentration camp. I stood in the reconstructed bunks, where hundreds of prisoners had been crammed like sardines. I walked through the doors where the boxcars were unloaded of their human cargo and then into the shower rooms, designed to execute hundreds of people at a time.[1] I saw the furnaces where bodies of those labeled "inhuman" by the Nazis were burned, and I wept over the mass graves. Beautiful landscaping offering an insufficient memorial to what lay beneath the ground. I met a survivor of Dachau, the tattooed numbers on his arm faded but still visible.

In the course of a morning, the Holocaust became real to me. No longer was it a distant, dusty event in a history book. No longer could I fathom approaching it as an intellectual challenge. I could respond only with horror. I was captivated by this question: How could the Nazis do this? Not Hitler and his advisers, but the soldiers on the ground and the people of the city of Dachau. How could they *all* become monsters who industrialized murder? How could they actively or passively endorse the genocide machine?

The best answer we have is as horrifying as it is dissatisfying: they became monsters slowly, one day after the next. The camp at Dachau was opened in 1933, about three months after Hitler was appointed chancellor of Germany. Its original purpose was to serve as a prison for political agitators.[2] At first, no one died at Dachau. But since the prisoners were deemed enemies of the state, they were systematically dehumanized: stripped naked from the moment they arrived and then subjected to daily acts of humiliation.

Several "accidental deaths" occurred, officially inexplicable. By October 1933, execution was authorized for sabotage, escape attempts, and "political agitation." Kristallnacht, the infamous pogrom against Jews throughout Nazi Germany, didn't happen until November 1938, when the camp had been operating for almost six years. Eleven thousand Jews were incarcerated there. The crematoriums weren't constructed until March 1942, nearly a decade after the camp opened. By the time the camp was liberated in 1945, SS soldiers had killed more than forty thousand people.[3]

My visit to Dachau made the Holocaust real to me. It also made the German soldiers real. I saw that they didn't wake up monsters. They weren't born evil. They became evil one day at a time—one decision to go along, one decision not to speak up, one decision to look the other way. They were everyday people like you and me who became villains one step at a time.

A Good Day to Be Bad

There's no question we're obsessed with villains right now. Antiheroes, reformed kingslayers, and outright bad guys rule the multiplex, the small screen, and the bookshelves. From *Gone Girl* to Loki, our villains insist that heroes aren't really good, and antiheroes are worth rooting for. Broadway's *Wicked* and Disney's *Maleficent* invite us to revisit the old fairy tales to see if the wicked witches are as wicked as we thought. Even Superman has normalized killing, because *dark, edgy*, and *gritty* are the watchwords of the day.

Maybe it's this generation of political corruption and religious sex scandals. Maybe it's the information age, giving us access to more sides of more stories than we've ever had. Maybe it's just good storytelling. But when the Joker is more interesting than the Dark Knight, it's worth asking why. Why are we so obsessed with bad guys?

Because we want to understand. And to understand, we need to hear the other side of the story. We need to see the world from the bad guy's point of view.

The technical term for the ability to understand another person's position is *empathy*. Empathy is an essential human practice, particularly in a culture that is increasingly divided. Once upon a time, the person across the party line was a friend and fellow citizen with whom I disagreed. Now he is the enemy, a threat to my very livelihood; compromise with him seems impossible. Once upon a time, a person who disagreed with me theologically was still a sibling in Christ. Today we write a blog post or fire off a tweet dismissing her as a heretic who has no place in the wide stream of Christianity.

Empathy takes practice, so what better resource than the Scriptures? The Bible is filled with villains—people who have been depicted throughout history as irredeemably evil. They are the murderous brother, the evil queen, the femme fatale, the ultimate betrayer, the devil. We give these villains about as much thought as the number of verses they get—that is, not much. We don't read them as real people but as monsters who exist only to threaten the heroes of our stories.

But the villains of the Bible were real people. They were born into sin as we all are; they were not more evil than the rest of us. I'm interested in the paths they walked. When Cain stood in that field, why did killing his brother seem like the best option he had? How could Delilah betray Samson? Why did Jezebel hate God's prophets so much? How could Herod order the deaths of the infants? Why did Herodias want John the Baptist dead? What did Judas really hope to gain by turning Jesus over to the authorities? And how could any being who has stood in the presence of the heavenly throne want to rebel?

These villains deserve more than a cursory reading. Certainly history has done violence to their legacies far beyond what they may deserve. We owe it to ourselves to practice some empathy for these devils.

So this book is an experiment in empathy. Each section begins with a fictionalized reimagining of biblical villain-making moments. The villains are the protagonists. The stories are not meant to be strictly historical—though I did the best I could. For several of these characters, the Bible is the only source we have, and some are no more than a footnote in history. We will explore these stories as acts of creative empathy. The goal is to cultivate some understanding of these individuals and to ask how anyone could do what they did.

After we revisit each villain's defining moment, we'll investigate the biblical text in more detail, tracing themes in the stories throughout the rest of Scripture. We'll also reflect on where these themes emerge in our own spirituality and how we might pursue a more faithful walk with God.

The goal of this project is to understand, not to exonerate. Empathy does not insist we condone the beliefs or behaviors of other people, but only that we see the world from their perspective.

Yet we don't want to do this. We want to assume that wicked monarchs and murdering brothers and betraying disciples and Nazi soldiers are fundamentally different from us. We want to declare with confidence, "I would never do that!"

And for the most part, we're right. The vast majority of us won't participate in genocide and won't murder even one person. But that doesn't mean the same seed of evil doesn't live in our hearts. Ultimately, this is why we want to understand the villains. We want to see how we might be walking the path they've already trod. Why? Because now is the time to turn away, while sin is still just a seed.

Bad guys fascinate us because we have a sneaking suspicion they're not that different from us. Perhaps, if we can learn some empathy, we might discover we're walking their path—just a few steps behind. We might be able to repent before sin blooms and we become villains in our own right.

1

CAIN

The LORD had regard for Abel and his offering, but for Cain and his offering he had no regard.

GENESIS 4:4-5

Now

Cain knelt in the dirt, his hand coming to rest on the stone. The smell of char filled his nostrils; what burned on the altar was not True Fire. He stood and watched in confusion as the carefully laid rows of wheat blackened under the crackling red dance. Neat stacks of peas on the slab smoldered, and then the pods were consumed, revealing green kernels now blackening. As panic mingled with incomprehension, Cain eyed the potatoes and pomegranates, always the last to catch fire. *Will these at least burn with the True Fire?* he wondered.

Perhaps. But never before had the wheat or peas of his offering failed to burn true. No sooner had the thought crossed his mind than the precise circle of potatoes and pomegranates surrendered to flame. As they too began to blacken, Cain could no longer deny this was mere fire burning on the altar.

He stepped back, took in the old stone of the altar, the joints of stone weathered with age. Though the altar was older than Cain himself, it stood tall and strong. Each stone fit tightly with the others, so he could feel no cracks or spaces. The family altar was as strong as ever. Surely it was not at fault.

Cain could not recall an offering ever simply burning. How many had he witnessed his father offer? How many days had he lived? Each time, the True Fire had taken the fruits of the earth. Of course Cain had seen food burn; he didn't take to cooking food as readily as he did to growing it. Charred grains were a sight, an aroma he knew well. But never before, in all the thousands of daily sacrifices his father had made before Cain became a man, had he seen charred grains on the family altar. Never—even after his father allowed him to offer the sacrifice to The Name for the family—had he seen the fruits blacken and crackle in tongues of flame.

His chest still swelled with pride when he remembered the first time he had called the True Fire from the altar. The carefully arranged fruits and grains had been consumed, and the presence of The Name had fallen on the family. Tears of joy had wet his cheeks, and his father had whispered to him, "You have done well, Cain. Today you have pleased The Name and made your father proud." His mother had embraced him, her cheeks wet. Since that day, Cain had summoned the True Fire countless times.

But what is wrong today? he thought as he cast about, a call to his father rising in his throat. As he turned, his eyes found the True Fire—and the call died on his lips.

The True Fire burned, but not on *his* altar.

The scent of roasting meat pierced the odor of charred grain as Cain began to make sense of what his eyes told him. A few paces below the crest of the hill, a lamb lay on a small pile of rock, ill-fit and loosely assembled. The rock pile—Cain could never bring himself to think of it as an altar—rose barely higher than the grass. And yet the lamb was consumed, burning true. Tongues of fire licked at the carefully butchered carcass, leaping and dancing impossibly high, exploding into a flurry of colors no ordinary fire could match.

For a moment, his confusion turned to ash, and Cain stood transfixed before the True Fire, as always. It was as though the flames burned through the fabric of the world, consuming the thing without burning it. Though he had witnessed True Fire countless times, the impossibility of it never ceased to captivate him. The lamb did not blacken, yet it was cooked. As the True Fire transformed the offering into smoke that rose into the heavens, so the presence of The Name descended on Cain and—he knew from long experience—on all who bore witness to the True Fire.

For those moments the True Fire burned, Cain imagined he could see the Garden his mother sometimes spoke of. The True Fire did not destroy but revealed. So it was with the lamb being consumed: though its flesh never burned, the flames ate it away, layer by layer until there was nothing left but the assurance that The Name was well pleased with this offering.

As the final flickers of True Fire faded from his vision, taking with it the presence of The Name, the figure prostrate on the ground before the makeshift altar drew Cain's gaze downward. His brother, Abel, was weeping silently in a private ecstasy so intense, Cain felt like an intruder. He staggered away from the rock pile in shock, turned, and stumbled toward Home.

Down the gently sloping hill, Adam was already sharpening the tools, preparing for the day's planting, though the family had not yet broken their fast. The square of his shoulders and the hard lines of his back shouted to Cain that his father had seen. Eve watched from the doorway, tears streaking her cheeks. Cain had seen pity often on his mother's face, but never for him.

With every step toward Home, Cain's confusion turned toward rage. He spared no glance backward to see if his brother had followed. The soft, joyful weeping told him that Abel still lay on the hilltop.

He remembered when Abel had built his makeshift altar several plantings ago.

Before

Cain had been making the offering regularly for several seasons. Adam still led most of them, but at least once every seven, he let Cain offer to The Name and let him be the first to sense The Name drawing close, the presence revealed by the True Fire.

Cain had been working alongside his father in the field, tilling new dirt, removing stones. Adam always remarked that if the earth grew crops as easily as it produced stones, weeds, and thorns, they would be living in paradise. The words had the form of a joke, but his father's eyes showed no mirth when he spoke them. After his own exile, Cain would realize this was as close as his father ever came to speaking of the Garden.

As usual, Abel was nowhere to be found. He didn't have the mind or the constitution for working the earth. If anyone had asked Cain where his brother was, he'd have shrugged and said, "Probably off counting sheep." Abel was the shepherd of the family.

But there was no one to ask after Abel, and Cain wasn't thinking about his brother. He was immersed in planting the seeds in the carefully tilled rows, perfectly spaced. Every season was important, and Cain gave careful attention to the growing and the harvest, but it all began here. The coarse, rocky soil did not easily yield crops, so over the seasons, he and Adam had learned how to wrest as much food from the earth as they could. Adam often praised Cain's work and followed him more and more to learn what came naturally to his son.

That day, Cain had caught Adam staring back toward Home and the pastures beyond. Adam often gazed toward the pastures, a resigned longing in his eyes.

When Cain followed his father's gaze, he saw Abel struggling under the weight of a stone. He watched as Abel staggered up the hillside toward the family altar, watched as he stopped near the top of the hill, watched him set it atop a small pile of others. The rock carrying had continued throughout the morning, followed by short periods of building.

They had gone back to planting, and eventually Eve brought the midday meal. She broke bread with Adam and Cain, and as Abel approached, she called out to him, "Abel, what are you playing at?"

Abel looked shyly at the ground as he lowered himself and grabbed a piece of bread. Unable to disguise the pride in his voice, he said, "It's an altar, Mother."

"We have an altar, Abel," Adam grumbled. "And you are not the eldest."

"I know, Father. It's not—I—I know. I cannot offer for the family. I only want to show my devotion to The Name."

Adam only grunted in response, and after the short meal, he and Cain returned to the earth, and Abel returned to building. Only a few days later, Abel made his first offering.

Now

As Cain drew near to Home, Eve reached out to comfort him. He shrugged off her touch and stalked inside to break his fast. As always, the fruit of his labor was bountiful and lay across the table. A loaf of bread crowned the center, surrounded by chickpea cakes. Several fruits and fruit pastes, sliced and arranged, radiated out toward each place setting. A bit of cheese rested in a small dish toward the foot of the table. Cain lowered himself to the table and tore off a piece of bread. He dipped it in apple paste and shoved it into his mouth without waiting for his parents to join him.

Then Adam and Eve did join him, breaking their fast in silence for several minutes. The pall of Cain's humiliation hung over the table, souring the fruit. His mother spoke up, offering the blessing, though they were nearly finished. "Adam, you are my husband. You are strong, as constant as the earth from which you came."

The silence descended again, Eve imploring Adam with her eyes. Finally he said, "You who were once bone of my bone, flesh of my flesh. You are my wife, you are the mother of life."

Freed to continue the ritual, Eve turned to her son, her eyes welling with tears, her voice trembling. "You are Cain, our son. In you, we know that when we return to dust, our life will not end."

At this, Cain erupted. "Enough, Mother! Did you not see? I am rejected."

Eve reached for him, her voice a plea that sought to deny his anguish. "You are not rejected, my son. Is your father rejected when you make the offering? Please, Cain." She began the prayer again, "You are our son. In you—"

Cain would not be placated. "I did everything right. My offering was perfect, as it always is. I spoke the words. But the True Fire did not fall for me. It did not fall on the family altar. It fell on the lamb, on that embarrassing pile of rocks. It fell for—" He was unable to finish. Anger swelled again, cresting over his shame. "The Name has rejected me. Does a prayer change that?"

Silence descended again over the table, and this time Eve did not move to finish the prayer. Finally Adam looked to the doorway and inquired, "Where is your brother?"

Cain pushed himself up from the table, his frame cutting through the silence as he stormed away. At the doorway, he snatched his hoe. He saw Abel, playing shepherd again with his little flock, laughing and leading them toward the nearby stream.

He spat back, "Apparently the offering was food enough for Abel." With that, Cain stalked toward the field.

At the table, the cheese sat uneaten.

Before

Adam and Cain had found the earth especially receptive to seed and were anticipating the most fruitful growing season in a long time. Cain rose early; truth be told, he had barely slept. He rarely slept much the night before he made the offering. By the time the rest of the family had roused themselves, he had prepared all the fruits and grains and placed the wood on the altar. A rare smile crept across Adam's face.

Cain led the offering, and the True Fire came at once, as it always did. The presence of The Name enveloped them all, as it always did. And they returned to break their fast, as they always did. Except Abel hadn't come with them.

After they spoke the blessing, Adam turned to Cain and asked, "Where is your brother?"

They rose from the table and looked outside. Abel knelt at his stone pile, and smoke was rising from the makeshift altar. Cain rushed out. *Is Abel burning more food?* As he drew nearer, the unfamiliar fragrance of roasting meat filled his nostrils, and his mouth watered even as disgust rose in his throat. Cain saw a lamb burning, consumed, and not revealed.

After his offering burned, Abel came in, his tear-stained gaze downcast. Adam said softly to him, "Abel, you did not offer on the family altar. You are not the eldest. You cannot summon the True Fire."

Abel smiled faintly. "I know, Father. I did not offer to receive the True Fire."

Confused, Eve prodded him. "Then why are your cheeks wet, Abel?"

"I am only sad, Mother. The lamb I offered was the strongest of those born this year. I had grown fond of him."

As it so often did where Abel was concerned, exasperation quickly replaced concern. "What now, Abel?' she asked. "How many more of these offerings will you subject us to before you choose yet another distraction?"

Abel murmured an apology. "The offerings are for The Name, Mother. I will make them after we break our fasts, so as not to disturb you."

They finished their meal in silence. Though as Cain was heading toward the field, he heard his parents' voices, already escalating into shouting. His father did not come to the fields for a long time that day, and they did not plant nearly as much as they had planned.

The next day, Abel made his offering alongside Adam.

Now

In the field, Cain worked alone. Behind him, the next row of rich, tilled earth was straight and true. Again and again, the hoe flashed in the sky. Again and again it cut into the soil. More often than not, the hoe struck a stone. After several strikes, Cain fell to his knees and removed the excavated rocks, dropping them into the lanolin sack slung over his shoulder. Always more quickly than he liked, the sack was full, so he walked to the stream to deposit the rocks near the waterway. During the times when the fields were fallow and when the work didn't consume their daylight, Cain and Adam used the stones to dam the stream and to repair the sheepfold or the home. Even the stones had their uses.

That day Cain's hoe cut deeper, his bag filled faster. Near midday, as he turned again toward the stream, his shadow burned into the ground, as though the sun had suddenly doubled. Shielding his eyes, Cain cringed even as the presence of The Name fell upon him. A figure stood before him, feet straddling his carefully tilled row.

Cain fell back, staggering several steps before falling to his knees. The figure standing before him burned with True Fire. Its multicolored tongues danced and licked the earth, running along his row before dissipating. Awe swelled in his chest, followed closely by fear as he felt the figure's gaze upon him.

"Mercy!" Cain finally croaked, his hands shielding his face. "Have mercy, Strength!"

The figure laughed. Its voice came as a whisper, and Cain heard in his bones rather than with his ears. "I am not Strength, Cain. Do not fear."

This figure looked to have stepped from his imagination, from the stories his mother had told him of the Garden, of the serpent and the fruit, of Strength and his flaming sword, barring them forever from paradise. As his eyes adjusted to the figure, Cain saw no sword. *But if this is not the Strength—*

Cain threw himself to the ground, the stone sack pressing uncomfortably on his stomach. "The Name!"

Kind laughter came again from the figure. "Get up, Cain. I am not The Name. Let us say I speak for The Name. You and I have much to discuss."

Cain rose carefully from the dirt. He tried again to look at the figure but found his eyes couldn't hold its image. It was shaped like a man, more or less. There was an impression of wings, though it may have been the True Fire licking and dancing about it. And waves of power flowed off the figure. Cain realized these were the source of his fear. They gave the impression of violence, of strength. It was not a threat, exactly—just raw power.

Cain straightened. "What does The Name wish of me?"

Kindness washed through Cain. "You are angry. The Name wishes to know why."

Stunned silence filled the air. The muscles in Cain's shoulders tightened. The whisper came again, "Why are you angry?"

Cain spoke, cold and hard. "Better to ask why The Name is angry with me."

"The Name is not angry with you. Did The Name not come to you this morning?"

"The Name did *not* come to me this morning," Cain spat. "The True Fire fell on Abel's offering."

"It does not matter on whom the True Fire falls. When your father makes the offering, do you not still experience the coming of The Name?"

Again the air between them filled with silence. At length, the angel repeated, "Why are you angry?"

Rage boiled in Cain. "Why did The Name not receive *my* offering? I was appointed to give this day. I prepared the fruits perfectly, as I always do. I gave them on the altar." Cain paused, his blood hot, his voice cold and razor sharp. His eyes searched for a hint of compassion, of understanding, but found only intimations and whispers. "I burned the fruit on the *altar*. Not on some pile of stones held together with a boy's folly."

"Why are you angry?"

Cain's voice rose now, his anger flooding over his natural stoicism. "I am Cain. By the sweat of my brow I have tilled these fields." His arms swept out, encompassing carefully terraced hills packed with perfect rows. He pointed to field after field, stabbing the air with his finger. "Where was Abel when I tilled this soil? Where was Abel when I planted that field? Where was Abel when we saved that terrace after the great storm three seasons ago?

"Where is Abel even now? He's not *here*. He's not working our fields."

Gently the whisper echoed, "Cain, where is your brother?"

Cain's rage churned within him like a storm. "Why does The Name care so much for Abel? If you want to find him so badly, follow the smell of the sheep."

"Why are you angry? If you do what is right, you will be accepted."

The storm of Cain's rage broke the levees of his restraint, flooding onto the field. "If *I* do what is *right*? I have done *everything* The Name asks. I have honored my father and mother. Do you think I can't see how my father aches for the pastures? Our fields are a prison to him, a reminder of his curse. Yet still I have made peace with the land. I have worked tirelessly alongside my father, learned his craft, imitated his every move. I have worked to make food by the sweat of my brow. I have labored against thistles and weeds while my brother does nothing.

"You say *I* will be accepted? I have made offerings as often as my father instructs. If that is not enough, if The Name prefers my brother, then go to him. Let The Name feast on lamb and cheese."

The figure did not move. If anything, tendrils of True Fire reached higher and wider, threatening to embrace Cain. And though kindness remained in the whisper, the laughter was gone. "The Name received your brother's offering today. What is that to you? Your family received blessing. You are not rejected. This day is as every other."

When the figure made no move to leave, Cain turned to stalk away, anger bleeding away, soaking into the earth in the wake of his explosion.

The whisper stopped him midstep. "Cain, you stand at a precipice." The angel was pleading. "Do you not understand? Death is crouching at your doorway. It seeks to consume you. Do not let it."

"I am Cain. No man or beast can master me." His voice was once again low, cold, and firm. "I am life for my parents. If The Name believes me to be weak, The Name is mistaken."

Then he realized he was speaking to an empty field. He turned to find the figure gone—and with it the presence of The Name. He had barely noticed its passing.

The Name thinks me weak? The Name prefers Abel, the child, the shepherd? Abel, who has not harvested a single crop? Abel who tills no earth, who splashes in streams with sheep while my father and I wrestle thorns and weeds and stones that we might live?

This Cain would not abide. He had never said a word when his mother and father encouraged Abel's frivolity. He built the sheepfold when asked. He ate the cheese, drank the milk when offered. He watched as Abel enjoyed the fruit of his labor: the breads and fruit made by the sweat of Cain's own brow. And never had he spoken a word.

Standing at the edge of the field, his sandals on the uneven, untilled earth, Cain saw his brother chasing the sheep across the pasture, laughing, calling to them. *For this The Name rejects me? Despite a lifetime of faithfulness, despite endless work? No.* Cain would not be rejected. He called to his brother and waved him over. As always, Abel was quick to obey. He left the sheep, hurrying to his brother's summons.

As he approached, Cain knelt in the dirt, his hand coming to rest on a stone.

2

YOU WOULDN'T LIKE ME WHEN I'M ANGRY

How Anger Might Be an Invitation to Life

I committed the sin of Cain when I met Tom.

No, I'm not a murderer. I wasn't in a field, and Tom wasn't my brother. But I committed that sin all the same. I was sitting in a seminar room on the third floor of the Arts and Science building at the University of Missouri, beginning my second year of graduate school.

Before coming to Mizzou, I had attended a small Christian college in Southwest Missouri. I studied religion, which meant each of my classes was filled with students who saw the world the way I did, more or less. We were all evangelical Christians.

But grad school found me at the University of Missouri, studying religion in a state college. I went from being one of a few dozen Christians in every class to often the only evangelical. In those first few months, I was anxious, intimidated, and overwhelmed. Many of my classmates had a background in secular religious studies and had already read many of the theorists and scholars we were assigned. I struggled as I never had in high school or college.

Within the first few weeks, the other students took to calling me the religion department's token Christian. One of them joked,

"Every religion department needs a token Christian student, and JR. is ours." Though it was a friendly jest, the nickname helped to ground me and give me confidence. As the "token Christian," I knew my role in the department. I didn't fear speaking up, offering my insights or opinions. It was suddenly acceptable for me to offer a Christian perspective, because I was the token Christian kid from the small, confessional liberal arts college who had come to the big state school to study religion.

Over that first year, I settled into my role as the token Christian and began to enjoy my studies. I was still challenged, still intimidated, but the new identity I had adopted provided a context in which I could act, think, and grow.

This brings me back to Tom and to my first class, year two. We began class by introducing ourselves around the table. Tom explained that he had recently graduated from a small Bible college in Northeast Missouri and had come to Mizzou to study religion with people who didn't share his worldview.

I hated Tom immediately. "What a jerk," I observed to a classmate later that day. My classmate was genuinely confused. Tom had struck him as a likeable, friendly guy. But I wouldn't hear it. As far as I was concerned, Tom was the devil.

I couldn't see it at the time, but I disliked Tom because he challenged my identity as the token Christian. Compared with the other students in our program, he and I had identical stories. He was me.

If Tom became as integrated into our program as I had become, I would no longer be the token Christian. And if I wasn't the token Christian, who was I? That identity had made it possible for me to navigate the program and had given me confidence to build good, healthy relationships with my classmates and professors. It had made it safe for me to learn the tools this very different educational experience was offering me.

Tom threatened all that. So I lashed out in anger, desperate to protect my status.

Identity Crisis

The same trajectory of sin that led Cain to murder his brother is one we can all walk if we're not careful to identify Cain's sin in our own lives and root it out *before* it manifests. What was Cain's sin? The obvious answer is murder; he killed his only brother. But *why* did Cain do it? The superficial answer is that he was mad because God accepted Abel's offering but not his. This raises another question: Why would God receive one's offering but not the other's?

Again, the obvious answer may not be the best. Abel gave the best of his flock, while Cain gave only some of his crops. That's the common answer in sermons and commentaries and Bible studies. But that obvious answer isn't obvious to the characters in the story. Cain didn't seem to have any idea why his offering was rejected in favor of his brother's.

Cain's anger blossomed from confusion and hurt over his rejected offering. In response to his anger, God didn't chide him but pleaded with him: "'Why are you so angry?' the Lord asked Cain. 'Why do you look so dejected? You will be accepted if you do what is right. But if you refuse to do what is right, then watch out! Sin is crouching at the door, eager to control you. But you must subdue it and be its master'" (Genesis 4:6-7 NLT).

God implied that Cain had not yet been rejected, which is confusing, given that Cain's offering was rejected. But if we take God at his word—that Cain had not yet been rejected—this conversation was an invitation to Cain.

Put yourself in Cain's sandals. Even in the opening of his story, he was the favored son. At his birth, his mother named him Cain, which means "strength" or "spear" in Hebrew. She chose that name because "I have produced a man with the help of the Lord" (Genesis 4:1). Abel's birth, on the other hand, is presented as an afterthought. Even his name, Abel, means "vapor," a word describing the morning mist burned away by the sun.

This story was told and written down in a culture in which the firstborn son carried the whole weight of the family, their past, and their future. He was their historian and their legacy. He embodied their hopes and allayed their fears. Cain was clearly this sort of child; even his name reveals that. Cain was strong. Cain was life for his family. Cain was future, hope, dreams. Abel, on the other hand, was a mist that's gone with the sunrise—an afterthought.

Firstborn. Most important. Carrier of our hopes. Cain had woven an identity out of those titles, those roles. As we all do, he came to inhabit his identity. Just as being the token Christian informed my place among my fellow students, Cain's role as the firstborn informed who he was in how he related to his parents, to his brother, and to God.

We all inhabit labels, which ground our identities in something. Some of us ground our identities in a relationship: I'm a faithful spouse or a productive employee. I'm a loving parent or a dutiful child. I'm a loyal friend or a peacemaker. These identities we take on help us to know our place in the world. They teach us how we ought to relate to the people we encounter. They give us confidence to act, to move, and to know and be known.

But according to the Scriptures, these roles don't make for reliable foundations. When we look to our identities to give our life meaning, they become idols. Andy Crouch described an idol as anything that "advances a claim about the ultimate nature of reality that is ultimately mistaken. And since the Creator God is the ultimate meaning of the world, an idol is a representation of a false god. Implicitly or explicitly, all idols represent a challenge and counterclaim to the identity and character of the true Creator God."[1]

Grounding our identities in anything temporal is dangerous precisely because our lives are fleeting. I built my identity around being the lone evangelical in a graduate program that lasted three years. As I age, three years is a shorter and shorter piece of my life. How foolish it was to build my identity on something so temporary.

This is the sin of Cain: grounding his identity in something other than God. When we ground our identity in a label we've assumed (or been given), it's only a matter of time until someone challenges that identity.[2] What if he's a better father? Or she's a better employee? What if their children are better behaved or more successful? What if I lose my spouse? What if another Christian shows up at grad school? What if God accepts my little brother's offering, not mine? Suddenly the label that gave us such security and confidence shifts beneath our feet. Though it's caused by the shifting sands of our ill-advised identity construction projects, we cast the blame outward—onto *them*, onto the person who challenged our sense of self.

It's no surprise that we react with anger; our reaction masks our fear of losing what makes us *us*. But the real problem isn't threats to our identity. The real problem is that we ground ourselves in what is unstable. It's not *their* fault. It's *our* fault. We built our identity on sand.

What if we have the Cain story backward? What if God isn't punishing Cain, but trying to rescue him? "If you do well, will you not be accepted?" (Genesis 4:7).

Cain grounded his identity in being first—firstborn, most important, carrying the weight of his family's future. God wanted to rescue Cain from this, to challenge him to ground his identity in God, not in his role in the family.

So God rejected Cain's offering but accepted Abel's. God forced "most important" to be "the other guy" for a day. God pushed on Cain's sense of self, and because Cain had grounded his self in sand, his identity shifted. And Cain got angry, like we all do when our identity is challenged.

Warning Lights

God's rejection of Cain's offering was not a rejection of Cain. After the offering, God pleaded with him to do what was right. God pleaded with him not to give in to the sin crouching at his door. God asked, "Why are you angry?" (Genesis 4:6). This makes it easy to assume Cain's anger was his sin. But anger is not a sin. Anger is a God-given emotion, and it has a place in God's very good creation.

Counselors call anger a "secondary emotion," which means it's always caused by something else. Anger functions to protect our identities. According to forensic psychologist Stephen Diamond, anger is "an assertion of the individual's most basic right to be an individual." We view anger as a negative emotion, but Diamond pushes back on that, observing, "Without this capacity for anger or even rage, we would be unable to defend ourselves or those we love when needed. To fight for freedom and what we truly believe in and value. We would be unable to face down evil, leaving us even more vulnerable to it."[3]

Anger is like a warning light on a dashboard. When we feel it swell in our chest, it's a signal letting us know someone or something is challenging our identity. So anger can be a sign that something is desperately wrong. It's the tightness you feel when someone you love is threatened; it's the heat that rushes to your face when you hear that human trafficking is happening in your town.

Anger is also irrational, such as the rage that bursts out when someone cuts you off in traffic. Or insults your favorite sports team. Or sends a perfect bento box to school with her kid every day. Or has the gall to choose the same graduate program as you.

Anger won't tell you what it's covering up. Is there a righteous cause? Or does it cover a hurt, insecurity, or trauma? Anger doesn't think; it only protects. It can't tell whether the identity being challenged is built on solid rock or on shifting sands. It knows only that something's wrong.

This is why, when we get angry, we need to heed God's warning to Cain: "You will be accepted if you do what is right. But if you refuse to do what is right, then watch out! Sin is crouching at the door, eager to control you. But you must subdue it and be its master" (Genesis 4:7 NLT).

Watch out! Your identity has been challenged!

Watch out! You're about to react right now, and your reaction has the potential to bring life. But if you don't get a handle on this, it will devour you.

Most of us *don't* get a handle on our anger. Either we let it burst forth or we bottle it up, tamping it down under shame and fear. Whether we blow up or bottle up, most of us don't acknowledge our anger. We treat it as a problem to manage rather than an invitation from God.

Anger is an opportunity to stop and uncover what's underneath the anger. It's a chance to dig down inside ourselves to look at the foundations and see what we're built on: rock or sand. God wanted this for Cain. God intervened in his world to invite him to a better life, a larger picture of *himself.* God wanted him to be free from the burden of being the firstborn, free from the burden of his family's history and future. God wanted him to be free to be generous rather than selfish. God wanted him to be—literally—a source of life rather than death.

No wonder God pleaded with Cain. And how tragic that Cain chose to cling to his shallow identity rather than let go and embrace the person God called him to be.

Another One Bites the Dust

Cain's refusal of God's invitation to stop and consider his anger had awful consequences—not just for him but also for his whole world. The same is true for us. We may not become murderers, but the cost of our anger can still be devastating—both to others in our lives and to us. In his Sermon on the Mount, Jesus warned,

> "You have heard that our ancestors were told, 'You must not murder. If you commit murder, you are subject to judgment.' But I say, if you are even angry with someone, you are subject to judgment! If you call someone an idiot, you are in danger of being brought before the court. And if you curse someone, you are in danger of the fires of hell." (Matthew 5:21-22 NLT)

Jesus' warning sounds a bit extreme. "You've always heard murder was bad, but I tell you even being *angry* with someone is just as bad!" Jesus is certainly using some hyperbole in this part of the sermon, but all the more reason to take his words seriously. How can a reasonable person equate anger and murder?

If anger is a warning light, an indication that someone is challenging my core identity, how I respond matters a great deal. As we saw in Cain's story, anger ought to be an invitation to pause, to consider exactly what identity is being challenged, and to decide if that identity is worth fighting for. Do you know what triggers your anger? Is it when you're driving or with a particular coworker or family member? What are the warning signs that you're getting angry? Do you find yourself tensing or clenching your teeth? Does your voice get an edge? Do you start to withdraw, or do you brace for a fight? Do your eyes turn green and your purple pants get tight?

If we can learn the warning signs of our anger, we can learn to pause, to take a break, to step outside the situation and hear God asking, "Why are you angry?" We can begin to determine whether our anger is righteous or reactionary. Then we need a plan for how to respond to anger. We aren't good at getting angry, so we need a practice regime. We need to call a time-out. Go for a run. Journal. Blast some loud music.

I'm an external processor, so I tend to wear my heart on my sleeve. My tendency is to blow up and lash out. So I've learned that when I feel anger settling onto me, I need to remove myself from the situation and give myself some space to think through why I'm angry. I dig down under that anger and figure out what's got me so worked up. And I make a plan to respond with love, grace, and truth rather than throwing stones.

Cain didn't pause. He refused to listen to God whispering through his anger. He refused to see his circumstances not as an injustice but as an opportunity. Cain the firstborn, Cain the number one had been reduced to number two. By accepting Abel's offering rather than Cain's, God had challenged Cain's perception of himself.

How wonderful if Cain had paused! Imagine if he had listened to God say, "If you do right, you will be accepted" (Genesis 4:7 NLT). Imagine if Cain had learned that his status had nothing to do with why God welcomed him. Imagine that Cain had seen that Abel's win didn't necessarily mean his loss—that God could accept *both* of them. Imagine if Cain had been able to see that his status as firstborn wasn't a position to exploit but a privilege to leverage for the good of his family—including Abel. Imagine if Cain had paused to realize that this God didn't respect position, that this God was the God of younger brothers and slave nations. And since this God—who created the heavens and the earth—is no respecter of persons and positions, *Cain* was the one who had everything upside down.[4]

But Cain didn't pause. He knew he couldn't attack God, but he wouldn't settle for being number two. So rather than allow God to change his perception and to reground his identity, Cain lashed out.

There's more than one way to be number one. God invited Cain to do what was right. Instead Cain killed Abel, making himself number one by default.

Cain embodied Jesus' warning to us: "You have heard that it was said to those of ancient times, 'You shall not murder'; and 'whoever murders shall be liable to judgment.' But I say to you that if you are angry with a brother or sister, you will be liable to judgment" (Matthew 5:21-22). When we're angry, we ought to pause and consider what part of our identity is being challenged. And we ought to consider whether that part is worth fighting for or whether we could instead reground ourselves in God and God alone.

Ghosts That We Knew

Tom challenged my "token Christian" identity, and I couldn't see it. All I felt was my anger. So, like Cain, I didn't pause and examine the root of my anger. I allowed my immediate dislike to fester. Tom and I were acquaintances, classmates, but not friends.

And my friends were right: Tom was a really nice guy. Over time, as he became part of our circle of grad-school friends, I couldn't help but like him. He was kind and humble and funny and smart. And to my surprise, his presence didn't cost me my place among my friends.

Over the next year, we became close—despite my antagonism. Today Tom and his wife, Cassie, are my best friends. Their children are our godchildren. Tom is also a pastor, and for the past decade he has pastored me and has been essential to my spiritual journey. He's walked with me through some of the most difficult moments in my life, and he stood as my best man at my wedding.

Had it been up to me, I would have missed out on this brotherhood. I cannot imagine my life without Tom. I don't know what sort of person I would be today, but I'm certain I wouldn't be the man I am. Yet that was very nearly the cost of my anger.

Jesus said that when we choose to hate rather than to pause, we're subject to the same judgment as when we murder. That's because when we respond out of anger, we cut off the other person's ability to challenge our identity. We allow her to be herself only insofar as that self agrees with us.

That denial of humanity is the sin out of which murder grows. And cutting other people off hurts me as well. If I don't allow them to challenge me, if I insist on protecting myself from anything that threatens my identity, how can I listen when God challenges me? Allowing anger to turn into hatred wounds my relationship with God, with my neighbors, and with myself.

Beneath the story of Cain is an ugly truth we're loath to admit: our identity *needs* to be challenged. We've all built our life on labels and identities that are not God's vision for us. And because God loves us, God pushes on those flimsy selves we've built. God challenges us and invites us to leave our crumbling life built on shifting sand.

God invites us as God invited Cain to ground our identities in Jesus, a solid foundation that will not shift, no matter what challenges life brings our way. When we build lives that do not rely on how others perceive us and what others expect from us, we find the freedom God intends for us: the freedom to love others. We also find the freedom to respond with generosity to our friends and our enemies. The freedom to celebrate when we have little or much. The freedom to work for the good of all, not just the good of us.

So the next time anger swells in your chest, remember God's warning to Cain: Why are you angry? You'll be accepted if you do right. But if you refuse to do right, watch out! Sin is at the door, eager to control you. You must subdue it and be its master.

3

DELILAH AND SAMSON

[Delilah] let [Samson] fall asleep on her lap; and she called a man, and had him shave off the seven locks of his head.

Judges 16:19

Beast

The monster slept, quiet as a baby, in Delilah's lap. Her slave slipped silently into the room, bearing her iron shears, blades freshly sharpened, then retreated just as silently. Carefully Delilah began to cut through the first lock.

It was not only that Samson was Hebrew. True, they were a backward people—a nation of shepherds, their pottery crude, their metal soft, their tales not even a millennium old. But they were a hospitable people, and Delilah had gained some wealth trading with them the fine Greek dishes she made. Besides, Delilah's own grandfather had been a shepherd.

The Hebrews may have been barbaric, but they followed the way of their god. Samson didn't fit even among the Hebrews. He kept none of their laws—eating from corpses, lying with foreign women. Samson was neither Philistine nor Hebrew. He belonged to a different age, one when the lines between things were blurred. Perhaps what the people whispered was true. Perhaps he was a demigod—Heracles himself stepped out of legend.

Delilah grimaced in disgust at the stench of Samson, earthy and unwashed. If he was half anything, most likely he was half beast. Men were creatures of reason, of thought and planning. This brute was a slave to his desires. He could do nothing but what his body demanded of him from moment to moment. It was fitting she sheared him as she would a beast. How fortunate he proved easy to domesticate.

Delilah tossed the first lock gently aside, then lifted the second.

Iron

Samson stirred. Delilah went still, not breathing, but he only turned and settled back into her lap. Delilah exhaled slowly. Her strongest wine had dragged Samson deeper into slumber.

The shears were sturdy iron, the blades honed to a keen edge. Despite their age, they were free of rust. Delilah kept the blades well oiled; they were all she had of her grandfather, of her childhood. She remembered the day they'd left Mycenae, the few animals that remained of her grandfather's once numerous flocks sold off to pay for their passage. But he had refused to sell the shears. Her grandfather had always boasted they were the first shepherds to use iron shears in their region.

But iron had not saved them from poverty. Delilah was in her seventh year when they came to Canaan. Her grandfather had not survived the journey, and her father had found the grapes growing in the Sorek valley. It turned out a Greek shepherd knew enough about winemaking to offer a vintage far superior to the native Hebrew fare. By the time Delilah became a woman, her father was wealthier than they had been in Mycenae.

Delilah had taken to their new vocation. She preferred the slaves who trod the winepress to the leering shepherds who had been in her grandfather's employ. She was happy to learn her father's business, happy to take it over after he followed his father into death. Wealth, she had found, outweighed womanhood in many matters, including wine.

Her lip curled into a sneer as she thought, *Wealth reveals what fools men are. Take it away, or have your own, and see them revealed for the petty, foolish creatures they could be. Wear no veil. Let them see a bit of your flesh and imagine your curves, and they can think of nothing else. You may take all you wish, and they will thank you for it. Rob them blind, and they will boast to their friends that they have the famous wine of Delilah's vineyard. Let them drink from beautiful Greek cups, and they will hate the crude mugs their wives and mothers made. They will insist you sell them cups too, and you will grow yet more wealthy, more powerful, by selling civilization to barbarians.*

Delilah regarded the iron shears again. *Wine that doesn't taste like vinegar they can have. Well-fired cups adorned with larks and storks they can have. But the secret of iron the Hebrews must not learn. Some among them are fearsome warriors—even those without the strength of gods. If they had iron swords and shields, my people might be chased out of our new home more swiftly than we fled Greece.*

Wedding

Even as a child, Delilah had heard of Samson. His village was no more than a morning's walk from her father's vineyards, and tales of his great strength circulated even then. He made a reputation as a brute—loud, selfish, thoughtless. He stole bread and sometimes vandalized a Philistine home. It was said he once carried off four sheep and held a feast for his friends. The lords of Philistia called him a troublemaker, though Delilah heard he troubled his own people as often as he did hers. He was a local legend, yet a minor, if irritating, annoyance.

But that was before his wedding.

Samson met his wife, Kala, on a journey to Timnah, the Philistine village closest to Hebrew territory. Her father owned the oldest vineyard in the valley. He had helped Delilah's father begin making wine, giving a gift of some of his own grapes. Both men made excellent wine and had developed something of a rivalry. Take as proof that their relationship remained friendly the fact that Samson had invited Delilah's father to provide some of the wine for Kala's wedding.

Delilah had grown up with Kala. Unlike Delilah, Kala had no nose for business; she hoped only to wed—perhaps one of the fine sons of the lords of nearby Ekron. When Delilah heard that Kala had met Samson, she could scarce believe it. Even less could she believe Kala's father would agree to the marriage. It was not as though he needed more Hebrew buyers for his wine. And surely he knew they detested the mixed marriage as much as his own people did. *Could he be impressed with Samson?* Delilah wondered. She had heard nothing of Samson's wit—only of his great strength. Only at the wedding did it occur to her that he must have agreed out of fear.

The wedding was seven full days of feasting. If the Hebrews did anything well, it was celebrating. Samson had arrived alone but for his parents, who looked shamefaced throughout the feast. He walked as though he owned the very earth and sky. And he was attractive—Delilah could not deny that. It was a raw, primal thing, the sort of appreciation she found for a beautiful stallion. Even freshly washed as he was, he still smelled of sweat and animal, as though he had scrubbed away civilization, leaving only his base self.

At Samson's arrival, Kala's father went out to greet him. Samson offered him no embrace and only demanded, "Where is my bride?" It was then Samson noticed the lords of Ekron—thirty in all. Though he noticed their swords, he only laughed and insisted the festivities begin. Wine was poured, and the feasting began. Delilah had never experienced a celebration more tense.

Near the end of the first night, a drunken Samson staggered to his feet and approached the men of Ekron. Several grabbed their swords, but Samson only laughed, harsh and cruel. "Put away your swords," he jeered. "I wish to make a wager. You Philistines think you're so wise, so solve my riddle for me. I'll give you till the end of the feast. Solve it, and I'll give you each two garments—one of linen and one so fine you'll wear it to the next wedding you sully with your vulgar presence. You fail, and you give me thirty of each garment. What say you, wise men of Ekron?"

Silence reigned for several moments before one of the eldest rose to the challenge. "The gods never thought to create a day for a Hebrew to confound Philistines. Give us your riddle, Samson. We'll give you enough time to enjoy your new wife before we solve it and leave you poor as a beggar."

Samson smiled. Drunk, he looked more fox than man. "Very well. Here is your riddle. Out of the eater came something to eat. Out of the strong came something sweet. What am I?"

Again, a confused silence. Delilah watched as the men began to whisper among themselves, growing more agitated and frustrated as they spoke. Samson turned his back as he offered a final taunt. "And let it be known I'll not have the cloaks you're wearing. I want something that hasn't had your stink all over it."

None but Delilah noticed Samson's bride cowering in the corner.

On the fourth day, Delilah was serving wine when Kala grabbed her arm. She looked exhausted, but Delilah also saw terror in her darting eyes. Kala pulled Delilah out of the tent and began weeping into her arms. The lords of Ekron had come to her and demanded she learn the answer to Samson's riddle. They had threatened to burn her and her father alive if she refused.

"But I can't get them what they want. Samson doesn't speak to me. He drinks. He curses our people. And he—" She broke down again, but Delilah knew men and their lusts. She pulled her friend up and said, "Men are stupid, shallow creatures ruled by their desires." Soon enough, Kala saw how she might gain the answer to her husband's riddle.

On the morning of the final day of the feast, Samson taunted the lords of Ekron again, reminding them they had only until sundown to answer his riddle. One of them stood and announced, "What is sweeter than honey? And what is stronger than a lion?"

Delilah watched Samson's face redden with rage, the muscles on his shoulders and arms tense and bulging. "No wonder my wife has had no appetite for me. This is not wisdom, but treachery! If you had not plowed with my heifer, you would not have solved my riddle."

The lord protested, mockery in his voice: "Come now, Samson. No one has shared your wife's bed; though as eager as she was to betray you, you may want to keep a close watch on her. No need to be so sour."

"Indeed. I am nothing if not honorable." Samson's calm voice did not match the hue of his face or the set of his body. "Please, remain. Enjoy my father-in-law's hospitality. I'll be back shortly with your garments."

With that, Samson left, the laughter of the lords of Ekron chasing him from the tent. They debated whether they should leave, but none could resist returning home with a trophy from the mighty Samson himself.

The sun had nearly set when Samson burst again into the main tent, carrying two large bundles of cloth. He threw them into the middle of the table of the lords of Ekron, splashing food and drink everywhere. "Here is the reward for your treachery!"

One of the men stood, a scarlet-spotted linen garment in his hand. He shouted, "This bears the sigil of Ashkelon!" The lords of Ekron dug through their new robes, finding them to be soaked in death.

They turned toward Samson, who shouted over them all, "I asked your brothers in Ashkelon for help showing my appreciation for stealing away my bride at my wedding feast. They were reluctant, but after we had words, they saw reason."

Another Philistine exclaimed, "You slew the lords of Ashkelon?"

Samson grinned, cruel as a jackal. "As I said, we had words. They were reluctant, but they saw reason. You boast of Philistine wisdom? Now thirty of your lords know the secrets of the grave. I have fulfilled my word. I ask you now, lords of Ekron, do you wish to have more words with me? Shall we find more lords who need new wedding clothes? Perhaps in Gaza or Ashdod? What say you?"

In the face of his raw fury—and holding the evidence of his violence in their own hands—the lords of Ekron looked away and said nothing. He turned to his father-in-law and spat, "I will not share my bed with these dogs. Keep your daughter. She is not mine."

With that, the beast stormed out, leaving stunned silence in his wake. The only sound in the tent was Kala's weeping.

Lion

Delilah grasped the fourth lock of Samson's hair and reflected on how much it resembled a strong rope. She thought this appropriate, since she was leading him like a sheep dog. *Or a goat,* Delilah thought with a grin.

Samson's eyes fluttered, and he mumbled. Delilah began stroking his face, his arm, his chest, whispering as a mother to a child. "Shhh, sleep now, Samson. Nothing troubles you. Shhh. Shhh."

How did the pounding in her chest not wake him? She was less than halfway through; if he stirred, he would surely kill her. *He is less a goat on a rope than a wild lion who makes his den among humans,* Delilah thought. But the lion settled once more in her lap, and she readied the shears again.

Am I not a daughter of Dionysus? She thought back to the times when she and Kala had been practically sisters, when her father was still learning to make wine. They would run through the rows of grapes, laughing, pretending to be Maenads drunk on their lord Dionysus's wine. At night, Kala's father would tell them stories of Dionysus, lord of the vineyards.

His favorite had always horrified both Kala and Delilah. A king had tried to ban the worship of Dionysus, so one of the king's trusted advisers—who was faithful to Dionysus—led the king to the woods. A group of Maenads, including the king's own mother, came upon him. They were deep in a divine frenzy, and thinking him a lion, tore him apart.

Looking down at Samson, asleep in her lap, Delilah finally understood the story. *I am a Maenad, and here lies a pretender, neither lion nor king. The Lord of Wine himself has given this burner of vineyards, this breaker of oaths over to me.*

Delilah set the blades to Samson's fourth lock. She remembered how attracting his attention had been no difficult task. He liked wine and Philistine women, and she was a Philistine woman who sold wine.

Captivating him had also been nothing. She knew men always want what they can't have, so she had merely ignored his advances. As he became more persistent, she demurred coyly. Because her father had passed, and she had no brothers, Samson could go to no one but her. He could not purchase her as he had Kala. And so every day Delilah denied him, Samson grew more determined.

He did not seem to recognize her, which she used in her favor. She pretended to be amazed by his great strength. Laughed at his attempts to be clever. Feigned interest when he explained how the world works, as though she'd never left her vineyard. Soon he had tied her rope around his own neck, and still he thought himself the master.

Once she had him ensnared, she began working toward finding the secret of his strength. In the midst of much oohing and ahhing, she exclaimed in a voice thick as syrup, "You must be stronger than Heracles himself. Which of the gods is your father? Are you the son of your god, Yahweh?"

He laughed at her. "You sound like a Hebrew. I hear them whisper that I am as one of the Nephilim of Noah's day. Would it please you, Lilah, if I were a demigod from your tales?"

She did not enjoy this pet name for her: *Lilah*, the Hebrew word for "night." Because his mother named him for Shamash, the sun, he thought his name for her quite clever. Men who believe they're cleverer than the women they want are on a short rope indeed. And in Delilah's experience, men always believed they were cleverer. So she smiled sweetly, laughed admiringly at his pet name, and demurred, "The truth would please me. Are you a demigod?"

He swore he was not, and Delilah sensed the truth in his words. Whatever the secret of his impossible strength, it was found elsewhere. This had been good news for her. She pestered him, careful to be playful at first and growing more petulant as he refused. Finally she sulked off, letting him chase her.

"Lilah! What does it matter where my strength comes from? Do you wish to betray me?"

Treading carefully, she concealed the truth within sensuality. "Yes, of course. Tell me how someone might bind you." She locked her eyes on his, and her wicked smile invited him to believe what he wished. "Someone wants to lay a trap for you."

He laughed, throaty and aroused. "Bind me with seven bowstrings that have not been dried yet—the newer the better. I'll be helpless before you." She knew it to be a lie, though there was a small seed of truth in it.

Acquiring the bowstrings was easy enough, and when she presented them to Samson, he grinned his wolfish grin and allowed her to bind him. She teased him, dancing about him. Suddenly she feigned fright and darted to another room. When Samson called after her, she exclaimed, "Someone is here!"

Quick as a panther, he was at her side, having burst his bonds like kindling. "What do you hear?"

She burst into crocodile tears. "My countrymen have come to kill us! I know it!"

By the time Samson had searched her grounds—finding nothing, of course—she had retreated to her bedchamber, far too traumatized for anything but sleep. The next day, rather than the hero's greeting he expected, Samson was greeted by the fury of a woman deceived. She would not speak to him, despite his countless apologies. Finally he said, "Bind me with new ropes. I'll be as weak as a woman."

For that last remark, she had smacked him, but playfully, her anger giving way to flirtation. She knew Samson to be lying still, but also that it was only a matter of time.

Again he broke his bonds; the new ropes were as threads around his arms. Again, false fury, apologies, and promises of restitution were the result. This time he promised, "If you weave these seven locks of my hair into a web, I'll be helpless."

This lie tasted more like truth than anything yet. Did the secret have something to do with his hair? Still Delilah was not surprised when he pulled away from the loom, alert and ready for violence.

Delilah was certain she was getting close, so she banished him from her home to let him pine at her gates for a day or two. Let him think he had lost her. Let his loins become yet more inflamed with lust for the fruit he had yet to taste.

In the meantime, she would send word to her employers, lest they think she had failed at her job.

Woman

Delilah was more than half done shearing the beast. She adjusted her grip on the shears and then lifted his fifth lock.

The lords of the Philistines had come to her only after Samson destroyed Gaza; they had failed yet again to defeat him with swords. They had hunted him ever since he murdered thirty lords of Ashkelon, though they feared searching too deep into Israel. Delilah was sure they were afraid of Samson himself.

No one had expected him to return for Kala, much less his rage when he learned her father had married her off. In retaliation, Samson tied torches to the tails of foxes and sent them fleeing with terror through the Philistines' crops. Kala's father lost his entire vineyard, and Delilah much of hers. Much of the grain surrounding Ekron burned, and the lords of the city were so incensed they killed Kala and her father in retaliation.

The rational part of Delilah knew they had seen this as the only way to hurt Samson. The friend, daughter, and sister in her swore vengeance on the man who had caused it all, the man who thought he drove Apollo's own chariot across the sky, the man who had decided long ago that anything he saw was his by rights.

The Philistines grew bolder or perhaps more desperate. They received word that Samson was hiding in Judah, so the armies of all five cities rode out in force to capture him. The Judahites were so terrified, they delivered a bound Samson to the Philistines. Samson slew a thousand men that day—some said with his bare hands and with a stolen sword. Some claimed it was a jawbone he ripped off a pack mule.

After that, Samson walked wherever he pleased. He turned up in Gaza, deep in Philistine territory, to visit a brothel of some renown. The men of the city arranged themselves in ambush, agreeing to strike at first light. Delilah wasn't sure what their plan had been—perhaps to confuse him in the streets of the city.

It didn't matter, because Samson finished with the prostitute and made his way to the gate, where he demanded they open it so he could leave. When they refused, he ripped the gates from their moorings and used them to demolish the watchtower and most of the wall surrounding the city. He left with the gates on his back, running as easily as a man might jog alongside his child.

Delilah heard the gates were displayed as a trophy in Hebron. Samson had run there that same night and delivered them to Judah as thanks for aiding him in his ruse against the Philistine army.

Not long after he destroyed Gaza, Delilah learned he had returned home. She had been surprised when the lords of the Philistines reached out to her. They knew she had caught Samson's eye. The lord of each city had offered her more than a thousand pieces of silver if she would tell them the secret of his strength.

Delilah didn't care about the money—though she would not refuse it. If they wanted to pay her to take her vengeance, all the better. She had decided to end Samson the very day Kala had died.

She considered the shears again as the fifth lock fell to the floor. *Fools, indeed. Swords are for men. Beasts require a different tool.*

Truth

Just then, Samson shifted once again in Delilah's lap, exposing the final two locks to her shears. She bared her teeth in a wolfish grin of her own. It was almost as though he wanted to be conquered. He was not stupid; even Delilah had to admit he was crafty. But like all men, he was a fool, a slave to his desires. She could not believe that he was wholly unaware of her goals. Yet in the end, he had told her his secret, as she had known he would.

She had sent for him—not that her messenger had to venture far from the vineyard to find him sulking about. When he came to her, she offered the petulant, churlish façade of a wounded lover. Before he could even reach her, she demanded, "Why do you say you love me?" She painted a thin veil of anger over hurt—and the hurt was painted over need. "If you truly loved me, you would tell me your secret."

Samson found the mixture irresistible, and within moments he was on a knee before her. "Lilah, forgive me. But why do you protest so much? You know I have been betrayed before. Should I not be suspicious that you gnaw at this like a—" He caught himself about to compare her to a dog and changed tactics. "Only my mother knows my secret."

"I care not where your strength comes from. But you do not trust me. You cannot love me if you do not trust me." Delilah thrust out her bottom lip in a pout to keep from grinning. "If you love your mother so much, perhaps you can share her bed tonight."

Samson sagged, and Delilah knew she had won. She remained silent, and finally he whispered, "A razor has never touched my head. That is my secret."

As soon as she heard it, she knew it to be truth. Now that his secret was out, she knew she must tread more carefully than ever. "You've never cut your hair? That's sillier than bowstrings or looms." Pouting, she added, "You still lie to me."

"I am a Nazirite." The wineskin opened, Samson could not stop the rush of words. "Before I was born, our Lord instructed my parents to consecrate me. No razor may touch my head. I cannot drink wine. I may eat nothing unclean."

Delilah allowed the shock to show on her face. "You are a terrible. . . . What did you call yourself? Nazirite?"

"The Lord did not consult me. Neither did my parents. The life of a Nazirite is a life of saying no." Samson grinned despite himself. "I like to say yes." He turned serious again. "The Lord is with me. That is the cause of my strength. My hair is the only thread of my vow that remains intact. Were it to be severed, I have no doubt the Lord would leave me. So that is my secret, Lilah. Now you know. And now you know that you have my love."

Delilah smiled sweetly and kissed Samson deeply. As he began to paw at her, she turned as though distracted and clapped her hands, summoning a slave. "Bring us wine and prepare a feast, but see we are disturbed by no one this night." Her smile promised Samson everything. "Tonight, we celebrate."

The slave returned quickly with the wine and assured Delilah, "All is as you commanded. Tonight shall be a night the two of you will always remember." As Samson laughed lewdly, Delilah thanked Dionysus. The slave remembered her coded signals, and word was sent; the lords of the Philistines would arrive in the dead of night. Now she had work to do.

Delilah poured her strongest wine into two of her most beautiful cups. She gave one to Samson and raised her own. "May all the gods bless this Nazirite."

He roared with laughter again and drank deeply. Delilah refilled his cup again.

That cup soon lay not far from his sleeping form, having been emptied many times before the beast finally collapsed into her lap.

Shorn

The shears slid over Samson's skull; he was now as bald as a newborn. She knew her kinsmen were there by then. Doubtless they were hiding in the next chamber, waiting for her to cry out.

Samson looked less beastly, and Delilah felt a twinge of pity. The Philistines would not be kind to him. Samson had humiliated them, emasculated them. Doubtless he would be humiliated, paraded before the people.

Delilah thought of the lords of Ashkelon, slaughtered for their robes because the fox was outfoxed. She thought of her father's vineyards, burned to the ground because this man could not be held accountable for his actions. And most of all, she thought of Kala, so innocent, so helpless, so frightened.

Delilah whispered into the beast's ear, "Wake up, Samson. Wake up!" He only stirred, so she slapped at his cheek, and he began to awaken. He knew immediately something was wrong, and his eyes widened as his hands felt for the locks that now lay on the floor. He turned eyes filled with horror toward Delilah. "What have you done?"

"Samson," she cried out, "the Philistines are here for you!" With that, a dozen men poured into her bedchamber. Samson threw himself at them, but he had told the truth; they easily overpowered him. He screamed and wept and shrieked.

Before he was dragged from her room, they gouged out his eyes and placed bronze shackles on him.

Delilah called for a slave to gather Samson's locks and burn them. That night she slept deeply, her dreams untroubled.

4

I'M NOT LIKE EVERYBODY ELSE

When the Light of the World Goes Dark

I wish I'd known my friend Becky Brown in high school. Becky was on the board of the church where I served in Beavercreek, Ohio. As we left the church building on Sundays, she would debrief the sermon with me. One of her favorite turns of phrase, always delivered with a smile and a sendoff, was "Holy means different, not weird!"

I was a weird kid in high school—partly due to adolescent awkwardness but partly because of the way I chose to inhabit my faith. I attended a public school, and I was committed to being a Christian in public. For me, this meant highlighting as often and as loudly as possible that I was a Christian. I argued with my biology teacher (who was a Christian) about evolution. I wrote papers and did projects on Christian themes. I wore Christian T-shirts that proclaimed loudly, "I BELIEVE!" My favorite read, "Don't Fight Naked!" on the front and "Put on the Full Armor of God" on the back, complete with an illustration and a tiny Scripture reference.

I had a chart proudly on display in my bedroom that helped Christian kids find church-approved music alternatives. Like Green Day? Try MxPx! Like 311? Try Pax217! Above all, I was a defender of truth, armed with my sword of the Spirit and stacks of apologetics books written specifically to help kids like me wage war, especially against godless science teachers who tried to force us to learn science.

Ironically none of that made me holy. I was a loud, brash brand pusher. Just because I wore a cross instead of a swoosh didn't mean I wasn't playing the same consumerist game as the kids at my school who wore Starter jackets, Mossimo shirts, or FUBU apparel. (Did I mention I went to high school in the nineties?) None of these behaviors marked my *character* as different from any of the other kids at my school. The ways I was religious looked suspiciously like the students who played football or did theater or had any other hobby. Christianity was just my brand. I couldn't imagine a holiness that was more than branding and behavior, so the faith I offered my classmates was nothing more than one more way to get through high school (and not a very appealing one). I could have learned a thing or two from Samson.

Hey There, Delilah

Delilah is the presumed villain of Samson's story. Her name is synonymous with the femme fatale, the woman who uses her sexuality as a weapon to destroy men. Her crime was seducing Samson to discover the secret of his great strength so the Philistines could destroy him.

But the book of Judges is not particularly interested in judging Delilah's actions.[1] Compare Delilah to Jael in Judges 4:17-24. Like Delilah, Jael was not an Israelite. Like Delilah, Jael invited a man into her bedchambers. Like Delilah, she immobilized said man by means involving his head. (She drove a tent peg through his skull.) Judges intentionally tells the stories of these two women to highlight their parallels. But Jael is a hero, while Delilah is a villain. The only significant difference is that Jael killed an enemy of Israel, while Delilah betrayed Samson, Israel's alleged champion.[2]

Samson, on the other hand, seems at first to be an unambiguous hero. He's Hebrew, one of the good guys. An angelic messenger announced that he was born to rescue God's people from the barbaric Philistines.[3] Samson had a superpower: impossible strength. He also had a secret weakness: his hair.

But as we read his story, it's hard not to see Samson through Delilah's eyes. He is proclaimed to be Yahweh's champion, but he never defended Yahweh's honor. He was uncivilized, brutish, and cruel. He picked fights he knew he could win easily. He showed blatant disregard for all his God's laws (except for his hair). He took whatever he wanted and was accountable to no one.

If you feel a little conflicted about Samson, don't worry. You're supposed to. He isn't meant to be read as a hero—quite the opposite. Samson was the last of the judges, which is the title the book of Judges confers on the various champions of Israel Yahweh raised up to rescue the Israelites from oppression. The whole book of Judges is one long downward spiral, and Samson was the rock bottom as far as judges go.[4] His was a betrayal of Israel's holy vocation, and for Judges, the ultimate sin. The book lays the blame for the tragedy of Samson and Delilah squarely on his shoulders. He's at best an antihero, and he makes a strong case for villainy.

Discerning the difference between the heroes and villains—between God's people and the Philistines—should have been easy. But it wasn't. Samson's sin was that he refused to live into his divine calling. Instead he did what was right in his own eyes, and all Israel followed him.

The Philistine Problem

Today *philistine* means "uncultured barbarian." We've taken the Philistines' biblical role as the enemies of God's people as an excuse to assume they were backward, ignorant, and dangerous—

little better than animals. But our image of the Philistines doesn't match the historical record.[5]

Exactly who the Philistines were is still a mystery. The best evidence we have is that they were a Greek seafaring people who fled the collapse of the Mycenean civilization around 1200 BCE.[6] Mycenea was one of the great Bronze Age civilizations in the Mediterranean. It was technologically advanced, participating in a commercial civilization that spanned the Mediterranean. Scholars debate exactly why all these civilizations collapsed at nearly the same time, but collapse they did.

The Philistines seem to be refugees who fled in waves to settle on the Canaanite Mediterranean coast. By Samson's day, they'd probably been a presence in Canaan for around a century. They established a network of five key cities known today as the Philistine Pentapolis.[7] They stood between Israel and the Mediterranean Sea, a recipe for a conflict as old as civilization.

What made the Philistines so fearsome? In a word, technology. They had entered the Iron Age, and Israel had not. Iron is much harder than bronze. Israel's swords and arrowheads could not pierce Philistine armor, while Israel's soldiers were extremely vulnerable to Philistine weapons.[8] Israel's chariots broke down more frequently and could not accommodate difficult terrain as readily. In essence, the Philistines were using smartphones while Israel was using the telegraph.

Far from being uncultured barbarians, the Philistines were civilized, educated, and well armed. They brought advanced technology and ancient beliefs and traditions to a land still embroiled in the aftermath of Joshua's conquest. They seemed invincible—until Samson came along.

No matter what the Philistines did, Samson defeated them. He took thirty lords of Ashkelon by surprise. He burned Philistine grain fields and vineyards, then killed the men who tried to stop him. The whole Philistine army massed against Samson, and he killed a thousand of them. Finally they tried to trap him in one of their great cities, but he ripped the gates apart, leaving the whole city vulnerable.

For the first time in more than a century, the Philistines had met a foe against which their numbers and technological advantage did nothing. They turned to Delilah, who soothed then slew the savage beast.

Though it's possible Delilah was a Hebrew, her actions reveal her allegiance to be squarely with the Philistines. That coupled with Samson's preference for Philistine women has led to a near consensus among scholars that she was a Philistine. As such, Delilah would have seen herself as cultured compared to the nearby Israelites. In her eyes, Israel was a barbaric collective of hill people still grasping for the technology and institutions her people had mastered a century or more before.

Most surprising is that Delilah is named in the narrative. None of the other women are, including Samson's mother, his wife, and the prostitute at Gaza. No men speak for Delilah, even when she conducts business. This indicates she was likely independently wealthy, which was out of the ordinary for Greek women but not unheard of.[9] The only other fact we know about Delilah is that she is from the same valley as Samson and his Philistine wife: the valley of Sorek. She would have grown up hearing whatever stories of Samson the Strong Man circulated. Even if she wasn't at Samson's wedding, she would have known of it after Samson destroyed the region's grain supply.

Of all the women in the story of Samson, Delilah is the only one he is said to have loved. But we know nothing of her motivations. Though a minority of scholars and storytellers wonder if his love for her was reciprocated, most assume Delilah wanted nothing more than Samson's destruction. Given his behavior in the story, it's hard to fault her.

Moon of My Life

From a narrative perspective, Delilah functions as harbinger of the end for Israel. Her name sounds like the Hebrew word for *night*, while Samson is named for the sun. He is day; she is night. In the framework of Judges, he is good and she is evil—or that's how it's supposed to work.

In the Jewish imagination, the boundaries God commanded between Israel and the surrounding nations are woven into the very fabric of creation. The seven days of the Hebrew creation story begin in a darkness described this way: "The earth was a formless void and darkness covered the face of the deep" (Genesis 1:2). The first three days of creation see Yahweh dividing, separating, forming. Yahweh spends the next three days filling those forms, so that the "formless and empty" becomes "formed and filled," and God's cosmic temple is ready for that first Sabbath rest.[10] God's final creation is the man and woman whom God commissions to rule as God's image bearers.

Later, at Sinai, God gives Israel a *torah*, a way.[11] In a sort of cosmic wedding ceremony, God makes Israel a holy people—set apart from the world. The torah created the people in the same way, forming them with boundaries and separation.[12] God intended this holy people to be a kingdom of priests (see Exodus 19:1-8).

The parallels are intentional: God creates a world and a people by establishing boundaries and identity. God also creates a cosmic temple in Genesis 1 and a tabernacle in Exodus, which is cared for by humans created in God's image and shaped by God's torah.

They are to be caretakers of creation and lights of the world. To be an Israelite is to follow God's torah to show the whole world the way to God. Israel's holiness is to be contagious.

Judges is the story of how the holy people failed to be holy. The constant refrain in the book of Judges is that everyone did what was right in their own eyes. Rather than follow God's torah, again and again they crossed holy boundaries to worship foreign gods.

As a Nazirite, Samson was to be the embodiment of Israel's holiness. *Nazirite* means "set apart." We know little about the day-to-day functions of Nazirites in Israelite culture, but we do know that they embodied the separateness of creation and of God's people. They were to abstain from wine. They were not to cut their hair. They were to be more diligent than the average Israelite about not eating unclean animals. Certainly they were not to marry foreign women.

Samson did all these and more, crossing again and again the holy boundaries that marked God's people as God's. The sun of Israel didn't shine God's light into the world, so the world was dark, and everyone did what is right in their own eyes. When Delilah finally appeared in the story, she was the unmaker. Through her actions, the man who took everything he saw was blinded. The light of Israel's sun went dark. Creation was unmade as God's champion was defeated. But his own appetites defeated him, not an outside force.

By the end of Judges, God's people had ceased to be holy. All the boundaries had been crossed, and there was no way to tell who was a hero and who was a villain anymore. The creative fabric of God's torah had unraveled, and Israel was effectively no more.

Early in Judges, when Israel still shined God's light into the world, a pagan woman named Jael saw that light and aided God's people. By Samson's day, the light was dark, so Delilah did exactly what we would expect anyone to do: she took care of her own people. She turned a profit. And as far as we are told, she felt no remorse. Why should she? She was never presented a better alternative.

This was Samson's failure: he refused God's calling to be holy, to be like God and unlike the world around him. The sun of Israel was called from birth to shine the light of justice and freedom but refused to shine. So the people stumbled in darkness.

Holiness in the Real World

Discerning what a holy life looks like in our modern world is no easy task. The instructions we find in the Torah are culturally bound. Today we wear clothes of multiple fibers, eat shrimp and bacon, go for a run on Saturday, get tattoos, and participate in a host of other activities explicitly forbidden by the holiness codes (see, for example, Leviticus 11:12; 19:19-28; Exodus 16:27-30).

That hasn't kept us from making new holiness rules, of course. My denomination, the Church of the Nazarene, has a manual with a section called "The Covenant of Christian Conduct." This covenant is our attempt to answer how we are to be holy in the world. For most of our history, our holiness code has been a list of don'ts: Don't drink alcohol. Don't dance. Don't go to movies. Don't go to the circus.[13]

I have a love/hate relationship with our covenant. On the one hand, it's important that holiness be a real-world experience. Holiness should not be confined to the sanctuary on Sunday morning or to a private prayer closet. Holiness is a public calling. I like that we put effort into imagining what holiness in the real world should look like.

On the other hand, modern-day holiness codes like ours tend to focus on behaviors rather than character. Where are our injunctions to embody the fruit of the Spirit? How might our churches be different if, rather than endless debates about alcohol, we pursued self-control as a virtue? What if we spent more time imagining together what kindness looks like or how gentleness is different from weakness when it comes to employing our God-given power in the world? What if we held up joy as a virtue to be pursued? What if we trained Christians to be peacemakers at home, in cubicles, and even on social media? What if we insisted on loving our enemies and welcoming strangers and refugees as though they were our own family?

Holiness is the key to our vocation. When we get holiness wrong, we cannot be the light of the world as God intended. But too often, rather than following God's way, we imitate the world around us. We have our own schools, our own bookstores, and our own music. In other words, we're not particularly holy. We do exactly what the rest of the world does, but we use *Christian* as an adjective, slap it on packaging, and call it sanctified. We train up culture warriors intent on legislating morality, so we're led not by pastors but by politicians who've grabbed us and use us for their own agendas. Rather than cultivating a reputation for looking like Jesus, we are known as hypocritical, judgmental, oblivious, shallow, antigay, and more interested in politics than in God.[14]

No wonder, then, so few people outside the church see anything good about the Jesus we claim to represent. Like Samson, we present no compelling alternative for those weary of the ways of the world. Yet also like Samson, we have incredible potential. Jesus himself called us "the light of the world" (Matthew 5:14). And Paul promised that the same Spirit that raised Jesus from the dead—the same Spirit that gave Samson his fearsome strength—is alive and at work in us, making us into the church and making us able to represent God to the world (Romans 8:11).

When I think of a holiness church, I think of the Bridge Café. My wife, Amanda, ran this little coffee shop on the campus of Wright State University for four years. It is owned and operated by the church we were part of in Dayton, Ohio. The church believed holiness is not fragile, but contagious.[15] They opened the café to create a space for university students to encounter Jesus.

No crosses adorn the walls of the Bridge Café, and there are no Bibles on the bookshelves. Rather than rely on objects of faith, the church relies on the manager to create a space in which the students can experience faith. During our time there, the café hosted events for students like Open Mic Nights, Poetry Slams, and the famous Free Weiner Wednesday on Tuesday, when church members volunteered weekly to grill and distribute hundreds of hot dogs to hungry college kids.

One of the great joys of that quirky little café was the question we got from the students, usually by their third or fourth visit: "Is this a Christian coffee shop?" We always affirmed that a church ran the café, but that it was not only for Christian students. I often inquired how they could tell, and their response was invariably the same: "I'm not sure. There's just something different about this place."

Students from all walks of life found a home away from home at the Bridge Café. Late-night conversations about life routinely turned to questions about faith, and that home away from home became a spiritual home. One of my proudest moments as a pastor was an Easter Sunday when my friend Nikki, then a dance major at Wright State, performed a dance she had choreographed as part of our Easter celebration. I had the privilege of baptizing her a few minutes later, and in her testimony, she shared how she had come to faith in large part because of how she had encountered Jesus at the Bridge Café.

God's way is beautiful and compelling. We were created to be God's image-bearers and to care for the world as God's representatives. We are called to live out God's way in front of the world around us. But like Samson, we can refuse God's call. We can instead do what is right in our own eyes, which often results in buying into the various visions of the good life our culture endorses. We become consumers, or we let fear determine our path. We treat pastors like celebrities or run our churches like businesses. These idols entice us from God's torah, and we cease to be holy. Without a holy people to shine God's light into the world, the world remains in darkness.

To be holy is to be the image of Jesus in the world around us, to be different in character, not only in branding. To be holy is not to wear Christian T-shirts and listen to Christian music.[16] To be holy is not to wage culture wars. To be holy is to be loving, joyful, peaceful, patient, kind, generous, gentle, faithful, and self-controlled. To be Christian is to seek peace with our enemies and treat outsiders like family. When we are truly different from the world around us in character, not only in behavior, we are a light shining in darkness. We are a sun that banishes the night.

5

JEZEBEL

As if it had been a light thing for [Ahab] to walk in the sins of Jeroboam son of Nebat, he took as his wife Jezebel daughter of King Ethbaal of the Sidonians, and went and served Baal, and worshiped him.

1 Kings 16:31

Dogs howled in the alleys below as Jezebul reached for the kohl. The queen of Israel began to apply dark lines to her eyes for the last time. In what was fast becoming a tired ritual, she cursed Yahweh and his meddlesome prophets. A tear leaked from her eye, and she was forced to start again. Jezebul banished thoughts of prophets. Instead she thought back to her last day as the princess of Tyre. It was the spring equinox, and her tutor, Ezermarq, had accompanied her to the festival and her betrothal.

Queen

The roar of voices announced their approach to the capital's main thoroughfare, and Jezebul peeked through the silk curtain of the litter. The streets of Tyre were packed with people darting like minnows among the stalls while merchants shouted over one another, each promising the best incarnation of what their competitors offered. After several moments, she fell back into the litter and remarked, "The crush of pilgrims never ceases to amaze me. Never is the city so full as on this day."

Ezermarq nodded and smiled. "All for the glory of Baal, Your Highness."

Jezebul laughed. "Yes, for the glory of the Lord, and plenty left over for Tyre herself."

"Jeze-*bul*! Jeze-*bul*!" The chant from outside told the princess they were nearing the Temple of Baal. Her mouth tightened as she grew both amused and frustrated. They chanted her name but did not call for her. Their cry meant, "Where is the prince?" This was the equinox, the climax of the spring festival. Throughout the winter, Baal had slumbered and the world died. Today his faithful called his name, waking him so that life may return to the world.

"Jeze-*bul*!"

Staring toward the chants as though she could see through the curtain of the litter, Jezebul spoke, "My brother is not fit to be king."

Ezermarq was silent for a moment then said softly, "Do not do this, Highness. Not again."

As though she had not heard, Jezebul continued, "Baal-Ezer is a sweet boy. He is kind and thoughtful. But he lacks the cunning a monarch of Tyre needs."

Some of the old authoritarianism crept into Ezermarq's voice. "Baal-Ezer is now a man, Highness. You attended his naming not a month ago."

Jezebul turned to glare at her former tutor. "My brother is not fit to rule. I am more fit for the throne by far."

Ezermarq was silent.

"I told my father as much. Do you know what he said? 'You are a woman. You are not fit even to be sacrificed.' Now that he has a male heir, I am useless to him. I wondered what would become of me. Would I be allowed at least to become a priestess to Astarte, to follow in his footsteps in that way if I cannot wear his crown?

No. Now I learn that I am to be given to the prince of Israel. Tell me, Ezermarq; what do you know of Israel?"

Her tutor shifted uncomfortably. "They are a young nation, Your Highness. But they show much promise."

Jezebul laughed, though there was no humor in her eyes. "You are too kind, Ezermarq. They are barbarians—a nation of shepherds with a jealous god. I am to be queen of the dunghill."

They traveled the rest of the way in silence, the clamor of the pilgrims their only company. Finally the litter stopped, and Jezebul's heart skipped a beat. She flung open the curtains of her litter to gaze upon the Temple of Baal, examining the stones a cubit across and pillars as high as three men, all white marble, smooth and polished. Gold leaf adorned the tops and bottoms of the pillars that flanked the building, towering over the mass of pilgrims. It was magnificent, even on a gray morning.

Jezebul thought of how it glowed in the sunlight, and despite her foul mood, she smiled to herself. *Where is my prince? Are we not here today to awaken Baal from his slumber, that he might bring life back to the world? Would not Baal himself soon chase away the cold of winter with the warmth of his light?* She stood at the center of the world to call the prince from his rest.

Jezebul's guard led her to the gates of the inner courtyard, passing priests dressed in fine purple robes expertly managing the throng of pilgrims. She was announced, and the gates were opened to admit her. She crossed into the inner court, and the gates closed behind her. The princess of Tyre paused to savor this sacred moment; it was as close as she would ever likely come to the glory of Baal.

Jezebul sighed heavily. The life of a priestess was a life of power in its own way. But her father had other plans. She prepared herself to meet him, Ithobaal, the king of Tyre. He waited on the very steps of the temple itself, standing with the high priest and two strange-looking men. The two were clearly foreigners—shorter than Phoenicians, with beards thicker than the current fashion. Their robes and jewelry marked them as royalty.

Jezebul noted that her father's royal guard stood well removed behind him, and across the courtyard from them were half a dozen foreign soldiers. Though their postures were relaxed, they scanned the courtyard as men well acquainted with violence.

As she neared, Ithobaal swept his arms open and approached. "My daughter, Jezebul, princess of Tyre and treasure of my kingdom!" A translator echoed her father's words as Jezebul stiffened in his embrace. She made her final plea into his ear. "Father, do not give me to this prince. Let me serve Tyre."

He whispered in return, "Be strong, princess. In this you serve our kingdom and our lord." His tone was thick with dark threats as he gripped her arm, compelling her toward the foreigners. Jezebul nearly looked back for Ezermarq, but she chose instead to imagine her tutor would not see her offered to savages.

Ithobaal gestured to the older of the men. "Here is Omri ben-Zuar, king of Israel and first of his dynasty—and the crown prince of Israel, Ahab ben-Omri. Jezebul, daughter of Ithobaal and princess of Tyre, here is your prince."

Jezebul smiled and declined her head demurely. "King Omri, may your reign be long, and may Baal protect you from the unholy sword of the usurper." She watched as the translator related her words in the barbaric Hebrew tongue and saw when Omri's eyes darkened with comprehension. He growled words that hardly needed translation, though the interpreter stammered, "His—His Grace King Omri had expected better manners from the princess of the great Sidonians."

Ithobaal's grip tightened further on Jezebul's arm. "My daughter apologizes, Your Grace. She seems to have forgotten the manners of court in the commotion of the festival. Women are so excitable. She meant no harm." He grasped her arm painfully, and his voice promised vengeance. "See now how excited she is for this union of our two nations."

Jezebul gave Omri her most radiant smile. "My father has the right of it. Allow me to apologize. I am but a woman, a shame to my proud people. Your Grace knows, of course, that Tyre has reigned in Baal's mercy for two millennia. And doubtless Your Grace, in his wisdom, is grateful for our people's many gifts to the world. He is aware, of course, that our greatest achievement is not our ships, nor can it be measured in horses and chariots. We gave the world the alphabet. The greatest minds of ancient Sumer and the wisest sages of the Pharaohs could do no more than draw pictures. Our people divided words into sounds and syllables, and so changed the world. Sounds and syllables, Your Grace."

As the interpreter rendered her words, the men exchanged uneasy glances. Before her father could cut her off, Jezebul pressed on. "For instance, change the first syllable of my name, and I am Balzebul—'Baal is husband to me.' Why did my father not name me so? Before he took the throne, he was priest to Astarte. Balzebul is a fitting name for the daughter of Astarte's priest. But I was born to no priest. No, I was firstborn to a usurper. A man who needed a dynasty—and quickly. A man who needed sons."

Her voice grew even stronger. "My father is no priest. And I am no son. So I am Jezebul, 'Where is the prince?' A prayer to a sleeping god. A disappointing child."

Ithobaal sputtered with rage, and Jezebul turned to face him. "More disappointing yet, my father had no sons. I was to be queen. But finally my father had a son who has just attained manhood.

Though he is a fool, he is a son, and so is more fit to rule than I. Now I am again the disappointment, of no more use to my father than to be traded for political favors.

"So I apologize, Your Grace, that my father thinks so little of your nation that he would offer you his shame. Perhaps it's because you so recently crawled out of the dung heap of barbarism. Regardless, you came here looking for an ally, but my father clearly sees in you only—what, Father? A buffer from the great Assyrians? Fodder for your wars of conquest?"

Jezebul could no longer feel her arm, and she braced herself for her father's wrath even as Omri's eyes flashed murder. But before anyone else could speak, Prince Ahab stepped forward, his eyes shining with mirth. He bowed deeply to Jezebul and in nearly flawless Phoenician said, "Your highness, forgive my brute speech, but would you not agree that though a father may have but one firstborn, all his sons are beloved? Israel can never match the glory of Phoenicia, but we are honored to call your people brother, to glean from your wisdom and your gods. I will do everything in my power to ensure Your Highness is most happy among our people. They will be honored to have such a wise and beautiful queen to lead our crude people into the light of civilization.

"As for our fathers, I am sure you would agree that both our kingdoms are most fortunate that men such as our fathers stepped forward to end the strife that would have consumed us and wounded our people. Your father slew Phelles, the would-be usurper who ruled but eight months. My father slew Zimri, the would-be usurper who ruled but a week. May Israel and Sidon both prosper under their rule. May their legacies be long and their friendship powerful. The Lord Baal grant it be so."

Ahab's words made peace. From that first moment, Jezebul had been captivated by him. She stood near enough to him at the ceremony to explain the winter rituals, and he joined in the liturgical chants: Jeze-*bul*! Jeze-*bul*! She found herself smiling as he shouted her name.

At the close of the ceremony, her father led the sacrifice to consecrate their betrothal. After Ahab left, she found her thoughts returning again and again to him. *Who is this cunning, well-spoken man? Who is this prince?*

A year later, Ahab returned to make her princess of Israel. She had not lived among the Israelites for a year before Omri died and she became queen. Ahab celebrated his ascension by building a magnificent temple to Baal in Samaria, and he brought in Tyrian engineers to ensure his new capitol was state-of-the-art. Jezebul found Ahab to be a fierce warrior and a brilliant politician. She grew to love him quickly, and he loved her.

Prophet

As Jezebul replaced the kohl on the vanity that held her makeup, she smiled grimly to herself. The Hebrews called the kohl *puk*. Change just one syllable—*purah*—and you have *winepress*. She thought with ire, *That Mot-cursed vineyard.*

If the queen of Israel had a black mark on her reign, it was the vineyard in Jezreel. Ahab wanted it, and the owner would not sell. Despite all Ahab's machinations, he was defeated and for days was inconsolable. Jezebul chastised him, saying, "You are king. Your subjects may not refuse you."

But for all their talk about kings, the Hebrews were inescapably tribal. Ahab explained that he was limited by the Hebrew god—that this god had given the land not to the crown or the temple, but to the tribes. The tribal allotments were sacred. The vineyard was not Ahab's by right, but Yahweh's.

Jezebul had not understood her husband's wisdom in this. She pleaded with him, berated him, shamed him. She pointed out that his god had stolen the land in the first place, so his king should be able to take what he wanted as well. She reminded him of the great songs of Baal, the mighty warrior who may not be refused. Still he pouted like a child.

So Jezebul had taken matters into her own hands. The elders of Jezreel knew to whom their position and wealth were owed. They did not hesitate to frame the vineyard owner and execute him on their king's orders. Within days, Jezebul had procured the vineyard for Ahab.

But somehow the prophet had found out—Elijah, the prophet of Yahweh. He had sneaked into the city and confronted Ahab publicly, declaring God's judgment for his theft of the vineyard. The truth had been a barely kept secret, and the prophet's righteous indignation had galvanized Ahab's opposition. Plenty of Israelites still feared Yahweh, and Ahab was forced to make a very public spectacle of his repentance to keep the peace.

Elijah. Jezebul cursed his memory then picked up her wig. As she carefully tucked errant strands of her hair out of sight, her mind ran ahead of her. Wig. *Sheitel* becomes with one letter *shetek*, or flood. Three years the prophet had shut up the heavens. Three years she had hunted him while he spread his filth, his intolerance. *Elijah has always been too small-minded,* she thought. *He imagines that his tiny tribal nation can cling to its tiny tribal god on the world stage.*

But she and Ahab were committed to bringing Israel and her people into power. Tyre was crumbling whether her father would admit it or not. Assyria and Egypt waned as well. If Israel could cast off her backward, isolationist god, it could become a leader among the nations.

Elijah told anyone who would listen that Ahab had abandoned the gods of his fathers. *Foolishness,* Jezebul thought. The land had belonged to Baal and Astarte before Yahweh stole it. She knew not how many of the Hebrews still worshiped the gods of the land. In any case, Ahab named his children Ahaziah, "Yahweh has taken hold," and Jehoram, "Yahweh is exalted." He worshiped Yahweh, but not Yahweh alone. Because he welcomed other gods too, Elijah had declared Ahab an unfit ruler.

What did Ahab do that the great Solomon did not? Jezebul cursed again. She did not care to spend her final moments with the prophet. But her mind raced around a groove worn too deep.

Elijah liked to call Jezebul the Murderer of Prophets. He had gone around insisting he was the only prophet of Yahweh left, implying she had killed all the rest. "Untrue!" she had exclaimed. Admittedly she had killed a small number of prophets who—like Elijah—refused to acknowledge that Israel had space for Baal and Astarte as well. Intolerance could not be permitted; it tended to flourish like a weed. But many prophets in Israel still spoke in the name of Yahweh.

Besides, who was the true murderer of prophets? Jezebul clenched her teeth at the memory of Carmel. She should never have allowed Ahab to leave her at the palace. After all, he and those Mot-cursed tribal elders had assembled with nearly a thousand of her prophets, none of whom had returned.

According to Ahab, her prophets had foolishly allowed Elijah to set the terms of the contest: whichever god answered with fire would be the true god of Israel. Elijah had allowed the prophets of Baal to go first.

"Jeze-*bul*! Jeze-*bul*!"

Four hours they cried out to Baal—to no effect. Elijah had let it go on, and as the morning faded with no response, he had begun to mock them: "Perhaps your god is sleeping? Wake him up!" And then he joined in their chant, mocking them with her name.

"Jeze-*bul*! Jeze-*bul*!"

Ahab admitted the prophet had laughed and laughed between his chants. "Where is the prince?"

Involuntarily she clenched her hands into fists as she remembered Ahab's account. Her husband had faltered, but she insisted he leave nothing out. He finally told her how Elijah's mockery had shifted, as he said, "Perhaps your god is relieving himself?" Then he began chanting, "Jeze-*bel*! Jeze-*bel*!"

Just one syllable made all the difference. *Zebel* in the Hebrew tongue meant "dung." "Where is the prince?" became "Where is the dung?" The people had understood; according to Ahab, they had laughed as her prophets screamed and Elijah taunted and Baal remained silent.

"Jeze-*bel*! Jeze-*bel*!"

After Elijah had contrived to have Yahweh answer in flame, he had instructed the elders to slay her prophets. Ahab stood by, impotent with the elders against him. They killed every one of her prophets. She raged in her mind, *And* I *am the murderer?*

None of her hatred for Elijah had accomplished its end. He had survived Ahab and her elder son, but not Jezebul. She wished only that she could have been there when he died. The people whispered that he was taken to heaven in Yahweh's own chariot. She often fantasized what an ignoble death must have taken the prophet for his disciple to tell such an outrageous story. *Was he taken by a fever? A snakebite? Did he suffer an accident helping one of the Hebrews?*

How she had reveled in the news that Elijah was gone. Had she only known. From Eli-*jah* to Eli-*sha*. She thought, *At least Elijah had been too stupid to do more than oppose them to their faces. He shook his staff and made a spectacle of himself, true, but the glow of a spectacle fades quickly in memory. Even his victory at Carmel gained him nothing.* She had brought in more prophets, and he had fled to the desert. Israel continued to worship Baal and Astarte alongside Yahweh and flourished under their rule.

Usurper

Jezebul frowned. Her eyes were still puffy, but that could not be helped. Satisfied with her appearance, she stifled her tears and summoned slaves to dress her. As instructed, they arrived with her royal robes and crown. Her remaining son was dead, so Israel had no king. When Jehu arrived, he would kill his people's queen.

She rubbed distractedly at a spot on the mirror. Spectacle tarnished far more quickly than good propaganda. She could not leave the palace without hearing that name whispered. *Jezebel.* Queen of Dung. If only the dead prophet's words were as forgettable as he was.

Jezebul had assumed Elisha would be an annoyance similar to his master. She was surprised to find him a cunning adversary. The people called him a prophet, but he seemed to fancy himself a king toppler, having already deposed the king of Aram. Now he had orchestrated Jehu's coup. Her son, Joram, the last king of Omri's dynasty, had been wounded on the battlefield. While he recovered at the palace, he left Jehu, his most capable general, in charge of the armies.

Jezebul had assumed Jehu was loyal. But Elisha sneaked into the army encampment and anointed Jehu Israel's new king. Jehu made for the palace, and Joram rode out to confront him. "Is it peace, Jehu?" her son had asked.

Jehu's reply had become a rallying cry for her enemies. "What peace can there be, so long as the many whoredoms and sorceries of your mother, Jezebel, continue?" Jehu shot her son in the back as he tried to flee.

Jezebul recognized Elijah's words in Jehu's mouth. *Whoredoms. Because I worship the gods of my father, I am a whore? Every son of Israel does the same. Am I a sorceress because I desired my adopted nation to be strong, to stand among the nations of Canaan as an equal? What magic do I work that the prophet and his lapdog successor do not? Jehu is as small-minded as the prophet who anointed him and the one he quotes. So he has toppled Ahab's dynasty. He will drag Israel back into the mud, undoing a lifetime's work Ahab and I built. Mot take them all.*

Through the tower window, Jezebul heard shouts as the palace gates opened. It was Jehu, coming to end the last of Ahab's dynasty. Word would reach her brother, but she had been right about Baal-ezer. He was not his father. He would send a strongly worded message and perhaps demand a tribute. But she would not be avenged.

The queen of Israel considered herself in the mirror for the last time. At a gesture, a eunuch brought her crown, and she placed it on her head. Jezebul stood at the window as Jehu rode into the courtyard. She spat at him, venom dripping from her voice. "Is it peace, Jehu?"

The man who murdered her son in cold blood would not meet her gaze.

"Is it peace, Zimri?"

He flinched at the name of the usurper but still did not speak.

"Where is your prince, Jehu?"

Jehu reached her window and called up. Even then he would not acknowledge his queen. "Who is with me? Who is with your king?"

Hands gripped her from behind. The queen of Israel closed her eyes as the window rushed forward.

> In the territory of Jezreel the dogs shall eat the flesh of Jezebel; the corpse of Jezebel shall be like dung on the field in the territory of Jezreel, so that no one can say, This is Jezebel. (Elijah, in 2 Kings 9:36-37)

6

HOUSE OF CARDS

Power, Fear, and the New American Gods

A friend once told me she had begun attending a church that used the King James Version of the Bible exclusively. I was surprised and inquired whether she struggled to understand the beautiful but archaic text. She replied without a hint of irony, "Our pastors are such good teachers, we don't have to read the Bible for ourselves."

I commented smugly that a pastor whose preaching encourages church members not to read their Bibles has no business pastoring. Fast-forward a decade or so. I'd been preaching full time for a couple of years, and I'd just delivered a sermon. One member of the congregation, a friend of mine who had a vibrant personal spirituality, approached me after the message. She raved about my sermon, how beautiful and brilliant it was, how helpful she found it—all the comments that stroke a preacher's ego. Then she dropped a bomb. Lamenting, she said, "I could have read that passage a hundred times and never seen what you explained in there. Listening to your preaching makes me think I shouldn't even bother reading the Bible for myself."

I was devastated. I wanted (and I still want) my preaching to invite my congregation to fall in love with the Scriptures, not to be afraid of them. I wanted my words to make the words of

Scripture come alive and seem accessible. But the way I was preaching was having the opposite effect. I had become just like those King James pastors, interpreting the Bible for my people so they didn't have to.

The closest I'll ever get to being a king is pastoring. We pastors stand on a platform raised above the congregation and tell people God's will for their lives. I'd be lying if I said that sort of power isn't enticing. It's the rush that comes on a Thursday evening, having dinner with some people from the church. Someone tells a story about work then looks at you and says, "But I thought about what you said in your sermon—" then they quote you. Then they say, "So I decided to respond like this." Pastor long enough, and people who trust you will quit their jobs because of what you say. They'll decide to get married or stay married or leave a marriage. They'll change how they parent their kids. That is power.

Pastors and politicians aren't the only people tempted by power. We all desire power at some level. Power is about control. It's how we impose our way on the world around us. Power is why we have conflict. It's not difficult to see how among seven billion people on one planet, each created to create, there's going to be conflict. What happens when the way I want to shape the world differs from your vision of the good life? What happens when the space I need to flourish overlaps and intrudes on yours?

The goal too often becomes empire: the imposition of my will, my vision of reality, on others. This is a neat solution to conflict. To preserve my way, my space, my ability to be me, I need to acquire more power—political, military, cultural. As long as I have more power than the "other side," I'm able to conquer them, to force them to become like me, whether they want to or not. My way, my vision reigns supreme. Throughout history, Egypt, Assyria, Babylon, Rome, the Mings, the Aztecs, and the United

States of America have enforced their visions of human flourishing on the world around them.[1] We wage culture wars, declaring ourselves queen of the cubicle or king of the castle.

Our bent toward building empires grows from humanity's original sin: acting as though *my* vision of the world is the one that will best lead to flourishing. Theologians call this attitude *pride.* Pride is at the root of every empire ever built, whether on the world stage or in an abusive home. And contrary to popular belief, pride is at the root of Jezebel's sin.

Bad Reputation

Jezebel is the prototypical evil queen. She is at once sexual temptress and ruthless monarch. Her name has become synonymous with the worst kind of woman. As I was growing up in a church, calling someone a "godless Jezebel" was about the closest we could get to cussing.[2]

The Bible presents Ahab as one of Israel's all-time worst kings, and his marriage to Jezebel is a case in point: "Ahab son of Omri did evil in the sight of the Lord more than all who were before him. . . . He took as his wife Jezebel daughter of King Ethbaal of the Sidonians, and went and served Baal, and worshiped him" (1 Kings 16:30-31).

"More evil than all before him" is not exactly a glowing endorsement of Ahab's reign. But the historical account gives us no reason to suspect Jezebel was unfaithful to Ahab (or that she somehow seduced him into marrying her). From a purely political perspective, Jezebel was far from a bad ruler. In fact, by some measurements, Ahab and Jezebel were among the most successful of Israel's monarchs.

Israel rose to prominence at a time when the Egyptian and Assyrian empires were both in decline. Israel occupied a desirable strip of land on the eastern coast of the Mediterranean Sea, and the relative weakness and internal turmoil of the neighboring empires allowed King David to establish and expand Israel's territory. Solomon further expanded and solidified Israel's borders through trade and alliances.

The alliances caused Israel's monarch problems with God. Political alliances in the ancient world were solidified through marriage. If two nations became family, there was less chance they'd go to war. Since the institution of marriage in the ancient Near East was polygamous, kings could literally have as many wives as they could afford (which is why Solomon had over seven hundred—plus all the concubines).

The queens didn't come alone. They brought their gods, not an uncommon practice in the ancient world. The hill country of Judea boasted plenty of high places on which their temples could be built. Building altars to other gods was what marked the kings of Israel as evil for the biblical authors.

As strange as it seems to us today, this question of queens and gods was a question of national security. The surrounding tribes and nations had no problem making alliances across nations; their gods complemented each other. But Yahweh, the god of Israel, was peculiar. Yahweh insisted again and again that Israel "have no other gods before me."[3] Yahweh insisted again and again that Israel didn't need any other gods. They didn't need a fertility god and a god of crops and a god of death and a god of the sun and moon and health and childbearing and war and—you get the idea. Yahweh insisted that all Israel needed in order to be safe and secure was Yahweh. Be faithful to Yahweh's torah, and Yahweh will ensure that you flourish.

Every marriage sent a message to the people: Yahweh is not enough. Yahweh cannot keep us safe. We need to ally ourselves with Moloch or Chemosh or fill in the blank of the next god Israel's kings bound themselves to for the sake of border security and happy allies.

Allies made Israel feel safe in a tumultuous time. Solomon's son Rehoboam triggered a civil war that split Israel into two countries: Israel (the ten northern tribes) and Judah (the two southern tribes). Conflict flooded the Promised Land for the next fifty or so years in a steady stream of wars, assassinations, and coups. Ahab's own father, Omri, took control of Israel's military after another general assassinated the newly crowned king and murdered his entire family.

From his father, Ahab inherited a crown and six years of peace. Yes, after half a century of constant conflict, Israel had peace. Ahab was determined to maintain that peace. How? According to Scripture, he set about immediately to "walk in the sins of Jeroboam," which is code in the book of 1 Kings for idolatry (16:31). Exhibit A for the prosecution of Ahab's sin is his marriage to the princess of the Sidonians: Jezebel.

Your Cheatin' Heart

The Sidonians were Phoenician. The capital city, Tyre, was ancient by Jezebel's day—nearly two thousand years old.[4] Phoenician culture was rich and proud. Their golden age began about four hundred years before Jezebel's day, around 1200 BCE.[5] By Jezebel's day, they were in decline. Though Israel was a relatively young nation, its influence in the region was strong. It made sense for the Sidonians to ally with the rising star that was Israel.

Though we call her Jezebel, her name was probably Jezebul. The name translates to "Where is the prince?" Before her father seized the throne of Tyre, he had been a priest of Baal. He named his daughter after a liturgical chant in Canaanite worship.[6]

Worshipers chanted, "Where is the prince?" to awaken Baal from his winter sleep.

So why "Jezebel"? The Hebrew word *zebel* means "dung." Someone—Elijah, another prophet, maybe the author of Kings—employed smear tactics as old as time to make his feelings of Israel's idolatrous queen known—from "Where is the prince?" to "Where is the dung?" As clever, cruel propaganda often does, the name stuck.

What did it mean for Jezebul to be queen of Israel? Her people were ancient and proud, living in cities for hundreds of years before Yahweh spoke to Abram, the wandering nomad. Her people were scholars and poets. They had given the world the alphabet; before them, cultures like Mesopotamia and Egypt used pictographic writing systems. She worshiped Baal, the ancient lord of the Canaanite pantheon. Israel worshiped Yahweh, a minor god with no land whose people had been slaves and shepherds, who had only in the past century crawled out of the primordial sea of tribalism to step into the civilization of monarchy.

Raised in the royal palace of a clever politician, Jezebul learned how to make a nation strong: conquest and alliance. In Ahab she found a worthy companion, a politician as skilled as she and a man who desired to bring his country into the modern age. Ahab built new cities, raised armies, and like all good kings of the time, made treaties with foreign nations. Ahab worshiped these foreign gods alongside the god of his fathers.

Did Jezebul see herself as committed to making Israel great again by restoring worship of Baal that Joshua and his conquest had driven out? Did she see herself as a progressive voice, challenging the lingering, backward tribalism and myopic faith of Israel? What must she have thought of Elijah, the prophet of

Yahweh who lived in the desert like an animal, wearing camel skins and eating bugs?

Ahab and Jezebul were a good example of an effective ruling couple in the ancient Near East. Under their rule, Israel knew peace for twenty years. After his death, Ahab's sons ruled under their mother's influence for almost another decade.[7] When Jehu assassinated Joram to end Ahab's dynasty, he also killed Jezebul, implying she continued to be a power behind the throne.

Jezebul was not a sexy temptress who seduced Ahab into sin. She gained that reputation in part because Israel's prophets compared idolatry to sexual infidelity. For Ahab and Jezebul, idolatry was their path to power. They desired power for the reasons we all do: safety and national security, the ability to make the world as they thought it should be. They ruled as they did for the good of the nation, for the flourishing of their people. They were convinced that their actions made for the best Israel. But they were wrong.

Give It Away—Now

Acquiring power makes sense, especially in a world of fear. If we're naturally going to clash over our ability to flourish, I have an obligation to me and mine to protect *us*—or to ally us with other us-es who can protect us all from *them*. Political philosophers call this a social contract. In his influential work *Leviathan*, philosopher Thomas Hobbes insisted that for humanity in its natural state, life is "solitary, poor, nasty, brutish and short."[8] His thinking has shaped Western culture ever since, from the US Constitution to Robert Kirkman's *The Walking Dead* and George R. R. Martin's *Game of Thrones*.

If Hobbes were right, our imperial impulse would be good. We should amass power to ensure we can impose our way on the world. But Hobbes is wrong. Our natural state is *not* "solitary, poor, nasty, brutish and short." When we live as though it is, we bend away from who God created us to be. We were created as holy stewards of God's very good creation. The sort of life Hobbes described, the way of living we see all around us, is not natural. It's the consequence of sin. Empire isn't the cure. It's a symptom of our disease.

Jesus warned that hoarding power will not gain us the good life. Rather we find life when we share power. In Mark 10, two of Jesus' disciples ask him for positions of honor at his right and left when he seizes power.[9] The other disciples overheard and got mad (that they didn't think of asking first), so Jesus lectured them:

> "You know that among the Gentiles those whom they recognize as their rulers lord it over them, and their great ones are tyrants over them. But it is not so among you; but whoever wishes to become great among you must be your servant, and whoever wishes to be first among you must be slave of all. For the Son of Man came not to be served but to serve, and to give his life a ransom for many." (Mark 10:42-45)

"You know how the world works. It's all power plays. They build empires like children playing king of the hill. *But that's not how it is among you*." The greatest in God's kingdom, according to Jesus, is the one who serves—the one at the bottom. In Jesus' kingdom, power flows in the opposite direction—not up to the person on top, but from the most to the least powerful.

In Jesus' kingdom, whatever power, position, and influence we have is to be used for the sake of the other—for them, not for us. Jesus repeatedly, stridently dismantled the categories of us versus them. Rich versus poor. Jew versus Gentile. Saint versus sinner. Even heaven versus earth.

Jesus' instructions about power are grounded in his own nature as the second person of the Trinity. God is essentially love, a love Jesus defines as the act of giving up the self for the good of the other.[10] God is essentially a being who gives for the good of the other.[11] God—the all-powerful creator of the universe—creates beings who are themselves creative. God gives power away, and the net result is *more* power, not less. This God—who we see revealed most fully in Jesus himself—does not hoard power, but shares it, even to the point of death.

Jesus summed up the whole torah of God, the way that leads to life, in one double-sided commandment: "Love the Lord your God with all your heart, and with all your soul, and with all your mind, and with all your strength," and "Love your neighbor as yourself" (Mark 12:28-31). Jesus' love is not a cheap, sentimentalized Hallmark kind of love. It is an insistent, persistent love that embraces lepers and prostitutes and Pharisees and Gentiles. Jesus' love is a bold love that stands against injustice, that isn't afraid to name sin, and that calls the marginalized to the center even as it calls the powerful down from their thrones. Jesus' love insists that the other is just as worthy as I am of love and grace and peace and flourishing, even when that other crucifies.

The Upside-Down Kingdom

Loving self-sacrifice is the essential way of God. Every letter of Moses' law points us to this fundamental behavior: love God and love the other. God has insisted since the beginning that this is the way to life, to flourishing.

In the name of security and prosperity, Ahab and Jezebel allied themselves with gods other than Yahweh. These gods welcomed child sacrifice and taught that humans were created to be the slaves of the gods, which translated into an oppressive, unjust society in which the majority were slaves to the priests and nobles. Israel's monarchs worshiped these other gods in the name of powerful allies, more secure borders, and sweeter trade deals. They made Israel just like the nations around them.

We may not be queens or presidents, but we still worship false gods who promise us life. They're not named Baal, Moloch, and Chemosh anymore. Today we bow to progress (which tells us we can save ourselves through science and effort), consumerism (which tells us we just need that new thing over there to be fulfilled), security (which promises a few more drones and guns, or maybe a giant wall, will keep us safe), and any of the host of other American gods.[12] These idols tell us the way to flourishing is something other than love of God and other.

We learn to resist the siren song of the American gods in the community of the church. If we are willing to follow Jesus' example of self-emptying, our churches can form us to share power like Jesus. Psychiatrist M. Scott Peck outlined the path to a sharing community in his book *The Different Drum: Community Making and Peace*. He calls this community "True Community." True community has four distinct stages of development.[13]

1. Pseudocommunity. The first stage, pseudocommunity, is the stage of small talk, of observations about the weather and recently released movies. People in this first stage avoid conflict, creating a positive space that doesn't have room for honesty or "negative" emotions. It *looks* like real community, but only because everyone is playing nice. Though the group is made of a bunch of others, we all pretend to be the same for the sake of getting along.

Pseudocommunity isn't inherently bad. We need an initial stage like this to lay the groundwork for true community.

2. Chaos. The second stage is—brace yourself—chaos. This is the classic "things get worse before they get better" stage. When the dam of false positivity breaks (and it will eventually), all those pent-up negative emotions flood out. Someone finally lets loose with her political opinion or complains about someone else's annoying habit. In this stage, all the others are finally expressing themselves, being who they actually are, and the us/them conflicts come to the surface. Peck calls this stage "beautiful chaos," because it's a sign of growth. The group members feel safe expressing themselves more authentically.

Unfortunately because we've all been told that conflict is bad, chaos is not usually resolved in healthy, life-giving ways. Instead most of us either leave the group or wait for the eruption of self to blow over. If the group chooses—as most do—to ignore the issues raised and simply pretend nothing happened, it returns to a state of pseudocommunity, ensuring that an eruption into chaos will happen again.

We've all been in churches, small groups, families, project teams, or relationships where this pattern happens over and over and over. Eventually these groups experience burnout and dissolve.

Fortunately a cycle of burnout isn't the only option. Instead groups can choose to move to the third stage: emptiness.

3. Emptiness. Peck observes that the barriers to authentic communication are behaviors and beliefs we can choose to shed for the sake of relationships. Emptiness is the most difficult stage, because it is a dying to self. We must set aside who we are and empty ourselves of our biases, prejudice, desire for control, mistrust, and more. We must choose to embrace openness, kindness, vulnerability, and extending the benefit of the doubt to others in our group.

4. True Community. Peck's final stage, true community, is possible only on the other side of emptiness. Only when all members of the group commit to emptiness can these disparate others begin to become a truly unified us—one that doesn't ignore significant differences, whitewashing the whole group for the sake of a shallow peace founded on suppression rather than flourishing. In true community, we're loved for who we truly are, not who we pretend to be. And we love others for who they truly are because we've learned that our differences make us better.

The emptiness required to reach true community is the loving giving away of the self that Jesus commanded us to imitate. When we introduced chaos back into God's perfect world, God did not leave us to our own devices. Rather, to quote Paul, who was quoting an early Christian hymn,

> Let the same mind be in you that was in Christ Jesus,
>   who, though he was in the form of God,
>   did not regard equality with God
>   as something to be exploited,
>   but emptied himself,
>   taking the form of a slave,
>   being born in human likeness.
>   And being found in human form,
>   he humbled himself
>   and became obedient to the point of death—
>   even death on a cross. (Philippians 2:5-8)

In Jesus, we witness divine self-emptying, the giving of self for the sake of all humanity. And Paul calls us to imitate Jesus: "let the same mind be in you."

American culture has entered a period of chaos in the last decade. The economic crash of 2008, the election of our first non-white president, and the rise of social media, among many other factors, have given more individuals in our culture a voice than ever before. Entire segments of American society that have been silenced and ignored for centuries now have the ability to speak to the whole culture. Chaos has erupted, often accompanied by vitriol and violence.

As a culture, we are in very real danger of working too hard to silence these marginalized voices, to shout them down or ignore them rather than do the difficult work of emptying ourselves. We do this by shutting our mouths and listening to the people with whom we disagree and by putting aside biases we have for the sake of trying to put ourselves in the other's shoes.

God left heaven and literally became one of us. The least we can do is work to see a political issue from our opponent's perspective. We must work to be able to say, "I understand," before we say, "I disagree."[14]

The church has a great opportunity in this age to model the self-emptying that is the very essence of God's love. If our people are gathering to worship across party lines, across social issues, across theological minutiae, if we are creating spaces where people are welcomed and loved such that they feel safe enough to allow the Spirit to lead them in the difficult work of transformation, then we will become a powerful force in our culture.

This takes practice. It takes a ruthless commitment to root out privilege, bias, and prejudice, and to be quick to listen, slow to speak, and even slower to become angry. But as we learn to follow Jesus in the ongoing act of dying to ourselves for the good of the other, we find true community. We learn to love not because we ignore the quirks and pretend differences don't matter. We learn to love *because* of our differences, because unity is not the same thing as uniformity.

What if Ahab and Jezebel had embraced this upside-down way God gave to Israel? How would Jezebel be remembered if she had leveraged her power and position for Israel as God commanded? Power doesn't automatically turn us into villains. Power is a good gift from God, given to be shared with those around us. We were created to walk the path of emptiness. We can avoid the power games that characterize so much of our world. As we are faithful, the Spirit makes us a light to a world tired of the poor and brutish stories we live.

7

HEROD THE GREAT

When Herod saw that he had been tricked by the wise men, he was infuriated, and he sent and killed all the children in and around Bethlehem who were two years old or under, according to the time that he had learned from the wise men.

Matthew 2:16

Herod the Great gazed upon the death of his kingdom. Perhaps a dozen figures cloaked in shadow stood behind the royal herald. Afternoon sun streamed through the windows far above, and lit candles decorated every fixture along the walls. Still, light did not quite reach the magi. Where their dark skin showed through their embroidered silk robes, Herod could discern inscrutable messages written in ink. Amulets hung from chains, and stones adorned every finger, hung from ears, and—Herod had no doubt—lay hidden in secret pockets and folds. Veils gave the only indication that at least three of them were women. Ancient power pulsed from the group, who stood silent, heads bowed in respect.

The herald cleared his throat, and though his hands shook, his voice did not. "May I present to His Grace the magicians of Parthia. They come bearing greetings from his august majesty Arsaces of Parthia, the twenty-fourth of his name, king of kings and lord of lords." The herald paused and glanced back toward the magi. Now his voice did shake. "These humble servants have come to pay homage to the newborn king of the Jews."

Herod stood slowly, his hand heavy on the golden lion that was his armrest so that his knees did not shake. He scanned the throne room, wondering for the hundredth time that day which of his courtesans were spies for Augustus. No eyes met his, of course. Who there was taking careful note of every word? Who would scurry from there to report to Rome all Herod said and did?

The king smiled wide and friendly down at the dark figures. "Welcome, beloved friends. I apologize for my herald. I will have him replaced with one who understands your beautiful language. I hear your meaning, and thank you for your visit." As the herald withered in terror, Herod gestured to the newly crowned prince. "My son and heir, Herod Antipas, thanks your master, Arsaces, for his kind consideration of us. Tonight we shall hold a feast in your honor, and of course we will celebrate the new prince of Israel."

As Herod collapsed back onto his throne, one of the magicians stepped forward. He cut off the herald's translation and spoke in perfect Aramaic. "Your Grace, the problem is not one of language." Frowning, Herod leaned forward in his chair. "I am Malchior, Your Grace, and we are well aware of the treacherous actions of your son Antipater II—how he tried to kill you and so was stripped of his crown. We wish your son Herod Antipas long life and health, but we have come to offer homage to the newborn king of the Jews."

Herod's smile slipped only slightly. The magi were uncharacteristically blunt for diplomats. Perhaps he could rid himself of them all the more quickly. "I apologize, friends, but there seems to be some mistake. No new king has been born."

Malchior was undeterred. He swept his arm in the air over his head, flashes of light trailing from his fingers. "Your Grace, the stars do not lie. We observed his star when it rose many months ago. Change is written in the heavens, noble Herod. So did our wise king Arsaces—may his rule endure forever—bid us to journey to you that we might offer the good will of Parthia to this king of Israel." As Malchior spoke, his voice became louder word by word, until though he did not shout, his voice boomed through the throne room.

Herod glowered. "Your tricks are impressive, Master Malchior. I have no doubt your knowledge of the skies is even more so. If what you say is true—and of course it is—we must consult our own sacred books. Would you give me leave to consider with my scribes? Please, enjoy the hospitality of my house."

Malchior bowed. "Might we offer to assist your scribes, Your Grace? Perhaps our knowledge can augment their search."

"Your journey has been long, my friends. You need not trouble yourselves with such a simple matter. Please, rest. I will send for you tomorrow." Herod summoned a slave. "Prepare quarters in Caesar's wing. Be sure they enjoy every hospitality we have to offer." *And,* Herod thought, *let them remember who I serve.*

Malchior bowed again, this time silent.

No sooner had they left the throne room than Herod hauled himself painfully to his feet. Antipas came to help him down the long steps, but Herod slapped his hand away and spat at him, "Fool! Assemble the scribes. All of them. In my private chambers. *Now!*"

As his son scurried away, the old king limped painfully down the steps.

Herod limped into his council chambers, hushing raised voices to whispers. He scanned the sycophants and hypocrites, chief among them his new high priest, Matthias. Herod gained his seat and asked, "What truth is there to this story?"

Matthias rushed to assure his king. "We have scoured the prophecies, Your Grace, and we see no reason to give these magicians any credence. The Lord frowns on sorceries and auguries in any case. Why would he announce this to the Gentiles but not to his own people? No, we should thank them and send them on their way."

"Fool," Herod spat. "I don't speak of prophecies. Has a Hasmonean usurper been born? Or someone of David's line?"

"No, Your Grace, nothing of substance. Just whispers and rumors."

"Fool!" Herod's tone was as cold as iron. "Rumors have destroyed better men than you.

"Tell me, Matthias. What will Augustus think when he hears a *rumor* that an envoy from his enemies in the East has met with us? What will the Caesar of Rome do when he hears a *rumor* that a new king of the Jews has been born, though I have told him nothing of the sort? Will these *rumors* put him in a merciful state of mind?"

Before Matthias could answer, Herod continued. "When Rome with her legions descends on Jerusalem from the west and Parthia's cavalry rides upon us from the east, will whispers and rumors save your wretched life and the lives of your wife and children?"

Matthias, white as his temple garments, stammered, "N—no, Your Grace."

"Then let us pray your foolishness has not doomed us all. Tell me what you have heard."

A voice called out from the back of the chamber, "The Messiah has been born. We should prepare the path of the Lord." It came from an old priest, nearly hidden by his fellows. His eyes shone with the unmistakable glow of religious zeal.

Others began to shout him down, but Herod slammed his fist on the table and demanded silence. "Who are you, priest? Tell me what you mean."

The old man shuffled forward. "I am Zechariah, son of Simeon, a priest of the order of Abijah. Like our father Abraham, the Lord did not see fit to grant me a child, even unto old age. And like our mother, Sarah, my wife, Elizabeth, conceived though she was advanced in years. A messenger of the Lord announced his birth and promised he was Elijah returned to prepare our people for the Messiah."

Another priest—one of Matthias's minions, judging from where he stood, tried again to shout Zechariah down. "We preferred your vow of silence, you old goat. Shall we hold a triumph for this so-called Messiah because you finally learned how to make a child?"

Zechariah did not rise to the bait, Herod noted. He only replied with the assurance of the prophets of old. "The Messiah has been born. Ask those who live in Bethlehem. We must prepare the way."

"Why Bethlehem?" Herod growled at Matthias.

"The rumors, Your Grace." Matthias glared daggers at Zechariah. "Some months ago, word reached us that a child had been born in Bethlehem. A child of David's line."

Herod's voice was a sword against the high priest's throat. "Why am I only now hearing of this?"

Seeing a chance to shift blame away from himself, Matthias blurted, "Simon was high priest then, Your Grace. He did not deem the information worthy of your attention."

"Simon was plotting with my treacherous son to poison me. Of course he withheld information about a child Messiah!" Matthias shrank back as Herod's voice rose. "But I installed *you* in his place for your loyalty to the crown. So why did *you* not tell me at once?"

Matthias sputtered apologetically, "Your Grace, by the time I was installed, the rumors had been investigated. We traced them to a group of shepherds who claimed to have received the revelation through angelic messengers." Matthias gulped.

Zechariah interjected again. "The Lord told the prophet Micah, 'You, Bethlehem of Judah, are by no means least among the rulers of Judah; for from you shall come a ruler who is to shepherd my people Israel.' The Lord promised Ezekiel that he would send a just shepherd to root out all the wicked men who exploit the poor and abuse his sheep." As he spoke, Zechariah looked squarely at Matthias. "Why should we be surprised that the Lord chose to announce the coming of this shepherd first to shepherds?"

Matthias turned to Zechariah and said with disdain, "They are shepherds. Worthless men. Who would believe they are heralds of the Messiah?"

Herod cut him off with a roar. "Enough! You are nearly as great a threat as was Simon. A small mercy that I am betrayed by your foolishness rather than your plotting. It matters not whether this messiah has been born. What matters is that people may *believe* he has been born. How did David take the throne from Saul? Because the people loved him. And how did Rehoboam lose the kingdom of his father, Solomon? Because the people were against him. How did noble Augustus defeat Mark Antony to take his rightful place as Caesar? *Because the people love him.*

"We have enjoyed peace for more than thirty years. And you think rumors of a child who is the Messiah do not deserve my attention? When this child has prophecies and rumors of angelic messengers behind him, you think I should not be troubled by this scrap of trivia?"

Herod found he had somehow gained his feet and was shouting, "I learn of this first when magicians from Parthia knock at the doors to my palace, claiming the very stars announced his birth? *This* is when you deem in your great wisdom that I should learn of it?"

Matthias cowered before Herod's legendary rage. He stammered, "Your G—Grace."

"*Out*!" Herod roared. "When I am ready to surrender my kingdom to fools and half-wits, I will call for you again!"

The priests and scribes left as quickly as they could. Only Antipas and his top general remained behind. Herod's rage cooled as the room emptied, and he turned to practical matters. "We must rid ourselves of these magicians as quickly as possible."

The general cleared his throat. "Your Grace, Parthia is strong, and a much closer neighbor than Rome. We should consider making this visit the beginning of a—fruitful friendship."

Herod turned to him. "Eliab, how is it my oldest friend speaks the words of a traitor?"

"Only a fool does not weigh every option. And my king is no fool."

Herod growled, "The fool is he who believes a choice between Rome and the whole world is any choice at all. We must let it be known in no uncertain terms that Herod is no friend of Parthia."

Eliab held Herod's gaze but nodded his assent.

"We have until the morning." Herod sat back in his chair and closed his eyes. "How can we rid ourselves of these troublesome magicians? And how will we deal with this would-be messiah?"

Herod sat once again on his throne. The herald announced the arrival of the magicians, his practiced pronunciation markedly more fluid than his predecessor's. Once again, the magicians stood shrouded in silence and shadow. Once again, Malchior stepped forward to speak for them, but Herod spoke first. "Great magicians of Parthia, we thank you for your visit. Clearly the wisdom of Parthia exceeds our own. At your behest, my wisest scribes have searched our holy books and have discerned that this newborn king of the Jews of whom you speak is our long-awaited messiah. We are greatly shamed that we who have awaited his birth so long have failed to welcome him. We wish to make amends. Clearly we have much to learn from a friendship with Parthia. Will you share your wisdom with us, that we might welcome our God's anointed?"

Malchior gave no indication that Herod's more conciliatory tone surprised him. He merely bowed and said, "Parthia is pleased to call Israel a friend. How may we be of service?"

"We know the Messiah is to be born in Bethlehem. It is a village not far from here. Its only value is as the ancestral home of our greatest king. Tell us, when was he born? When did his star appear?"

"The star appeared nearly two years ago, Your Grace. Thank you for your help. We will set out for Bethlehem immediately."

"Might I ask one further kindness of you?" Herod forced himself to remain relaxed as he laid his trap.

"Of course, Your Grace. How might Parthia be of service?"

"When you have found the child, return here and tell us how we too might go and worship him. Israel has been too long without her true king."

Malchior bowed again. "It will be as you say, Your Grace."

After the magicians left, Herod looked at Eliab. The general nodded and said, "My two best spies await them in Bethlehem."

"Good." Herod did not notice how his own voice shook. "If we cannot lay hands on the child before word of the Parthians reaches Augustus, we are finished."

Herod limped once more into his council chamber, where Eliab stood waiting for him. The old king gained his seat and dismissed his cupbearer. Once they were alone, he snapped, "What news of Bethlehem? It's been nearly a week already."

Eliab scowled. "The magicians are not in Bethlehem, Your Grace. Neither have they returned to Jerusalem. I believe they have returned to Parthia."

"No!" Herod hurled his goblet at the general. Eliab did not acknowledge the assault nor that the goblet fell well short of him, splashing his sandals with wine. "Did I not tell you to send your best spies?"

The general's scowl deepened. "The two I sent after the Parthians are the finest in Israel, Your Grace. I trust them both with my life."

"That seems to have been a mistake," Herod growled ominously.

"Your Grace, they are magicians of Parthia. Did you honestly expect we could spy on them if they did not wish it? Did you expect we could demand anything of them they were not willing to offer? We know not how they escaped, save that it was by magical means. We know not where the child is, but Bethlehem is a small village. We will search it. We will discover the child. I'll begin a discreet investigation."

"No." Herod's anger gave way to fear as he traced out the implications of the magi's betrayal. "If the magicians found this messiah, his family will flee at the first sign of danger. We cannot afford discretion."

"Very well, Your Grace. I'll have the child brought to you immediately."

"No. It is too late for that. If the emperor's spies have not already sent word to Rome, they will soon. We must leave no doubt we belong to Augustus."

Herod was silent for a moment. "How many boys with two years or fewer do you suppose live in Bethlehem?"

"Surely no more than six or seven, Your Grace."

"Seven boys." Herod barely hesitated. "Kill them all."

"Your Grace?"

"You heard me. Kill every boy two years or younger in Bethlehem. What is better: seven boys today or seven hundred when the legions of Rome descend on us? Go and kill these boys. Let the wailing of their mothers announce to Augustus we have no love for Parthia or their magicians."

"Yes, Your Grace." Eliab paused as he turned to leave. "Do you think it's true? Has the Messiah been born?"

"It makes no difference." The old king's voice was iron, and he tightened his weak grip on his chair. "What hope has the god of Abraham, Isaac, and Jacob against the might of Rome? Messiah or not, this child will die—for the good of us all."

8

BETWEEN ROME AND A HARD PLACE

Living in a World of Impossible Choices

One of my favorite films is *Gone Baby Gone.*[1] It's a noir detective story that illustrates a truth we don't like to admit: sometimes there's no good decision. Private Detective Patrick Kenzie and his partner/lover Angie Gennaro are hired by the family of four-year-old Amanda McCready, who has been kidnapped. They quickly learn that Amanda's mother is a drug addict and destitute. She loves her daughter but is too wrapped up in her own life to provide a stable home.

As the case twists and turns, Patrick and Angie ultimately find little Amanda safe and sound in the home of a couple whose own daughter had been kidnapped and killed as a child.

Patrick and Angie face an impossible choice: Amanda has been kidnapped and clearly should be returned to her birth mother. But her life would be far better if she remained where she was, with two adoptive parents who not only love her but prioritize her. Both options are right, and both options are wrong.

The lack of a good choice is precisely why many people don't like noir as a genre. We watch movies or read books to escape from reality. We want to live in a world—even if it's just for a couple of hours—in which we know who the good guys are and that they always win. Noir forces us to acknowledge that reality is rarely as clear cut as we wish.

The impulse to avoid the gray shades of reality is why we don't read Herod's part of the Christmas story when we gather to sing "Silent Night" and light candles. We can't imagine celebrating the birth of Jesus alongside the deaths of Bethlehem's infant sons. But for Matthew, Herod is integral to the story of Jesus' birth. He wants us to view Herod as a corrupt, foolish king, the antithesis of what a true king of God's people should be. Between the lines of Matthew's story, the real Herod peeks through. If we look closely, we see a king who feels trapped in an impossible situation, a king who marshals all his considerable cunning to find a way out.

Déjà Vu All Over Again

Why does the appearance of the Magi trigger such a violent response from Herod? The traditional nativity scene features three well-dressed men, often of indeterminate ethnic origin, holding little boxes of gifts. The so-called three wise men gather at the manger with the shepherds and the Holy Family, come to worship newborn baby Jesus. Both shepherds and kings kneeling before the God of the universe lying in a manger is visually striking, but nearly every element of our depiction of the magi is made up.

For starters, the Bible never says there were three of them—they brought *three gifts*, but they are not numbered.[2] Further, they don't appear in the manger scene because they don't arrive in Judea until Jesus is two years old. Our nativity scenes are a composite: Luke's framework—the manger, shepherds, and angelic choir, with the good bits of Matthew's story squeezed in.

So who are these magi? Matthew tells us they were "from the East" (Matthew 2:1). East of Israel was Parthia, the heir to old

Persia and an empire that caused Rome no end of trouble. The word *magi* comes to Greek from Persia, where it referred to the priestly caste of the Zoroastrian religion. Part and parcel of their work was reading the stars. Hence, when Herod asked the purpose of their visit, they told him they were looking for the newborn king of the Jews because they "observed his star at its rising" (Matthew 2:2).[3]

The three wise men of our nativity scenes seem to have been envoys from Parthia. They read in the stars that a new king of the Jews had been born. Parthia was anxious to capitalize on the regime change, so they made preparations for the thousand-mile journey. The magicians arrived in the capital city, Jerusalem (where else would one seek out a newborn king?), only to discover that the current regime had no idea what had taken place. Their presence generated a good bit of confusion at the palace.

Herod, for his part, had seen this before. The first forty years of his life had been constant warfare as the independent Israelite Hasmonean dynasty imploded.[4] His father, Antipater, was an adviser to the last Hasmonean king. During the Hasmonean civil war, Antipater appealed to Rome, which swooped in to quell the conflict in the person of the great general Pompeii.

It was 63 BCE. Herod was somewhere around ten years old when Pompeii's legions breached the walls of Jerusalem and broke into the temple. Pompeii himself entered the temple, trampling the holy of holies. For Herod, raised Jewish, such an act would have been unthinkable. God's holiness was dangerous even to Jews.[5] God's holiness was most concentrated at the temple, in the holy of holies (a very Hebrew way of saying "the holiest place"). Inside the holy of holies dwelled God's physical presence on earth. Even the Jewish high priest could enter only once a year, on the Day of Atonement.[6] Any Jew would be devastated to see a Gentile trampling the holy of holies. Pompeii the Great, general of the Roman legions, sent a clear message: Yahweh is no match for Rome.

Herod grew to adulthood in a world of shifting allegiances and constant war both in Israel and in Rome. After Julius Caesar was assassinated in 44 BCE, Rome fell into a civil war between Brutus, Cassius, and the Roman Senate and the alliance of Mark Antony and Octavian, Caesar's adopted son and heir. Antony had become impressed with Herod, so he named Herod the king of the Jews and charged him to bring Israel fully under Rome's control.

Because Herod's parents weren't Hasmonean, Herod knew his claim to the throne was weak in the eyes of the Jewish people. He divorced his first wife, Doris, and banished her and her son, Antipater II, so he could marry Mariamne I, a Hasmonean princess. In 37 BCE, he defeated his final enemy and became king of the Jews in name and in practice.[7]

Herod's victory would mean four decades of peace for Judea after twenty-five years of near-constant warfare. But unrest in Rome threatened Herod's crown. After Antony and Octavian defeated Brutus and Cassius, they tried unsuccessfully to rule together—Octavian from Rome and Antony from Egypt.[8] Their conflict devolved into war yet again, and Octavian emerged triumphant in 31 BCE. Octavian declared himself Caesar Augustus and set to putting his empire in order. This was bad news for Herod, who owed his kingdom to Antony.

Before Augustus could return to Rome, Herod rushed to meet him at Rhodes, and in a quintessential display of his political savvy, he threw himself on Augustus's mercy. Augustus knew Herod had been close to Antony, and rather than denying it, Herod embraced his fierce loyalty as his best quality. He offered that loyalty to Augustus.

Augustus was impressed by Herod's cunning and audacity, and confirmed his kingship. Because Judea was one of Rome's easternmost provinces, Augustus depended on Herod to keep Judea stable and quiet. The worst thing Herod could be was incompetent. Actually, incompetent was the second-worst thing; the worst would be treasonous. Augustus had offered Herod a second chance, and Herod knew he would not get a third. He spent the rest of his life loudly affirming his loyalty to Augustus.[9]

If Jesus was born around 6 BCE, as most scholars think, Herod was nearly seventy years old when the magi arrived. Their arrival threatened the fragile peace Herod had maintained through sheer force of will. He was not going to surrender that peace or his throne without a fight.

The Gift of the Magi

The Parthian envoy sought to put a king friendly to their interests on the throne in Jerusalem. Parthia had done this before: Herod won his kingdom from Aristobulus II, who was put on the throne by the brother to Parthian King Arsaces XXII, who ruled at the time of Jesus' birth. Herod's victory had been part of a larger conflict between Parthia and Rome, with Mark Antony leading Rome's armies in support of Herod.

Whether Augustus had spies in Jerusalem or not, Herod was certain he did. He was certain Rome would know of the magi's visit. At minimum, Augustus would think Herod was collaborating with Rome's enemies, and Herod would be dethroned and executed as a traitor. It was also possible that war could erupt between Rome and Parthia. That war would be waged over Israel, which was caught between the two powers as before.

How could Herod respond? He positioned himself as a potential ally of the Parthians, discerned from his scribes and priests where the Messiah was said to have been born, then sent the magi on their way with a promise to return with a full report. When they failed to return, Herod "was infuriated" (Matthew 2:16). He surely wondered how long the news would take to reach Rome and how Augustus could possibly view the unfolding of events as anything but betrayal and collusion with the enemy. Herod's last chance was to act decisively and publicly by sending a message that he was Rome's man to the end.

The population of Bethlehem at the time of Jesus' birth was around three hundred, which means the total number of male children two years old or younger would have been six or seven.[10] Seven children were weighed against Herod's own security. The lives of seven children were weighed against the life of a nation. For Herod, this was no choice. He had watched his father, brother, and friends die. He had executed his beloved wife and three of his own children for plotting against him. What were seven nameless boys he would never know?

Like many of Israel's kings before him, Herod looked to other gods than Yahweh for both personal and national security. Herod's allegiance to Rome was strong. His fear of Rome turned him into a monster; idolatry always has that effect.

Herod lived in difficult days and felt as though he was in an impossible situation. He'd spent his whole life negotiating among Rome, the Jewish people, Parthia, other neighboring countries, his family, his ambitions, and more. But in the end, the way he chose to negotiate left him the one true villain of the Christmas story: the king of the Jews who was so far from God that he not only missed the birth of the Messiah, he also tried to murder him.

Like Herod, we don't live in a world of easy choices. We find ourselves caught between impossible commitments. In a world that's all shades of gray, every choice feels like a compromise.

So how can we be sure we're not following in Herod's footsteps? In a world that's all shades of gray, how do we choose between bad and worse?

Slipping Through the Cracks

Even with this window into Herod's life, we struggle to imagine how he could order the deaths of children. But as a nation, we also trade the lives of children for security. In Pakistan alone, by 2014, the drone program pioneered by President Barack Obama killed an estimated 142 *children* while in pursuit of twenty-four suspected terrorists. Only six of those men were killed in those drone strikes.[11] And that's just in Pakistan and just until 2014. We are quick to vilify Herod for ordering the deaths of seven boys in Bethlehem, but most Americans give no thought to the US drone program that has been killing children and calling it collateral damage for the better part of a decade. We praise our drones as the next level of warfare, as sensible, and as in the best interests of national security. When we weigh the lives of faceless children living halfway around the world against our own peace of mind, and we choose to feel safe, we are most certainly following in Herod's footsteps, not God's.

A deeper problem is that the vast majority of us are only vaguely aware that the United States and her allies wage drone warfare. We have no idea of the price we pay for our sense of security (and it is only a sense, given that drone warfare has not demonstrably reduced the threat of terror in the countries where it has been utilized). Pakistan may as well be a latter-day Bethlehem, ignored and overlooked as a meaningless backwater country. And while her children die by the dozens, our ears are deaf to the laments of their mothers, much as Herod refused to hear as Rachel wept over her children (to paraphrase Matthew 2:18).

Like Herod, we have more urgent, more immediate concerns than faceless strangers half a world away. Unlike Herod, our struggles are much more ordinary. We're not torn between Rome and Parthia. We negotiate commitments to work, family, faith, and self-care. How do we take enough vacation? Exactly how many activities can our kids participate in before we go insane? Churches don't help the situation, filling calendars with activities, Bible studies, Sunday schools, small groups, and worship gatherings. Between sports leagues, ever-abundant school activities, and a little homework squeezed between the cracks, families with children feel stretched thinner and thinner—especially single parents, who face a workload that has increased dramatically.[12] The outlook isn't much better for those without kids. Gone are the days of the forty-hour workweek. Adults employed full-time work an average of forty-seven hours per week, with almost four in ten workers logging more than fifty hours weekly.[13]

Our culture's solution is *balance.* As Herod sought to balance the demands of Rome and his Jewish subjects, so we seek a healthy work-life balance. How do we balance family and friends? How do we balance faith and the rest of our lives? We feel like jugglers tossing ball after ball into the air, working desperately to keep them all moving. It's no surprise that in our increasingly post-Christian culture, church attendance is one of the first balls many choose to drop.[14]

Thinking like this demonstrates that we've commodified the life God has invited us into. We've reduced the resurrecting power of the Holy Spirit to an object, a component. Our religion sits on the shelf next to weekends on the lake and kids' activities and sleeping in one day a week and everything else that competes for our time. No wonder this shallow, privatized religion has nothing to say to bereft mothers across the globe. No wonder our dull, lifeless worship gatherings so often lose out to the life that is waiting everywhere else.

Reducing God to a commodity is idolatry. Balance can't be the answer to idolatry. As long as we're trying to balance God with anything, we've reduced the Creator of the universe to an object. When we concern ourselves with keeping everyone happy and in balance, the most vulnerable slip through the cracks. When we're focused on everything, the least get overlooked. Balance can't be the answer.

Fortunately Jesus doesn't offer us balance. Rather he offers us an entirely new way to see our lives. In John 12, Jesus reflects on his death with a paradox: "Those who love their life lose it, and those who hate their life in this world will keep it for eternal life" (John 12:25).

Our English translations make Jesus' words more confounding by translating two different Greek words as "life." The first two references to life are the Greek word *psyche,* which is often translated "self." It's where we get the word *psychology*. The last word, the "eternal life," is *zoe*. Think of psyche as all the stuff that makes up our lives: our identity, our goals, our ambitions, our struggles and failures and successes, our possessions, our families, etc. Think of zoe as the essence of life, the state of being *alive*.

Too often we treat religion as psyche. God is one more thing among a bunch of other things we have to shuffle and arrange to make sense of ourselves. But God is the very ground of our existence. God is the creator and sustainer, the source of zoe. When we reduce zoe to psyche, we are left aimless with no one and nothing to order our way, no means to make sense of our world.

Author and pastor Shane Hipps asks us to imagine zoe as a one and all the stuff that makes up our psyche as zeros:

> The value of zero and one is determined entirely by their sequence. If you put a zero in front of a one, it does not change the value of the one. If you put three zeros before a one, it does not change the value of the one. You could put a million zeros in front of the one and it does not change the value of the one. The value of the one will stay a one. Likewise, the value of the zero will remain zero in all these instances. However, if you place the one in front of the zero, suddenly you have ten, add three zeros after the one and it's a thousand. As long as the one is placed first, every zero you add increases the value of the one and the zero. Get the sequence right and the value of both is transformed in powerful ways.[15]

The stuff that makes up our lives is not worthless. God cares very much about our jobs and our families and our dreams and our hurts and everything else that comprises our psyche. But they are not what gives our lives meaning. The one—the *zoe*—God is the ground of our lives. When we try to put anything else in God's place as the origin and source of our lives, we devalue everything.

Our psyche is not our zoe. The stuff of our lives is not life itself. To forget that—to place anything in God's place—is idolatry, and God promises it leads to death. When we allow God to order our lives, we cannot help but notice the most vulnerable. We notice them because they matter to the one ordering our lives.

Gone Baby Gone (to Mexico)

While I was a pastor to young adults, I met Jenn Holden. She and her friend Sarah were college students who frequented the Bridge Café while I worked there. They became fixtures of the café, and we spent many nights having long conversations about life, faith, and the world.

During one of these conversations *Gone Baby Gone* came up, and Jenn and Sarah expressed interest in watching the movie. Always excited to introduce people to media I love, I arranged a watch party, and on the weekend a small crowd of us gathered to watch the movie. As the film ended, Jenn's sobs filled the room. She was devastated and left quickly to be alone with her thoughts.

A couple of days later, we sat down to discuss her reaction to the film. She spoke passionately and at length of her love for abused children, her anger at the parents and systems that fail to protect them, and her own feeling of inadequacy in the face of such terrible evils.

I listened for a long time and then challenged her to consider that her passion may in fact be a sign of God's calling on her life. Over the next three years, Jenn continued to grow in her faith and education. When she graduated, she took an internship in Monterrey, Mexico, with Back2Back Ministries, an organization that supports orphanages and works to provide educational opportunities for orphans as they age out of the system. To no one's surprise, Jenn stayed on full time after her internship, living in Monterrey for several years. She still works for Back2Back today.

Jenn is an example of what it looks like when our zoe orders our psyche. She is an example of what it looks like to attend to the most vulnerable. When facing impossible odds, she chooses to be present. She can't fix the problems of every orphan in the world—none of us can. But she heard the voice of God calling her to come and *be.* To live with the children who broke her heart. To let the love that flowed out of her brokenness become a fountain of living water in a dry, loveless desert.

The crisis of orphan care in our world is an impossible problem. None of us can solve this worldwide epidemic. But like Jenn Holden in Monterrey, we can be present. We can refuse to ignore the most vulnerable among us. Faithful presence, not balance, is the answer. Whether we're in a cubicle or a coffee shop or cheering on the sidelines at a Little League game, or even in a church pew, God calls us to notice and be present with the most vulnerable.

How might the Christmas story look different if Herod had trusted God rather than Rome? Might our nativity scenes include a grizzled old king kneeling next to those magicians? In the most detailed carvings, perhaps we could make out the tension on his face—the fear of Rome's power battling his fledgling hope in Yahweh's promised Messiah? His future is uncertain, but his present is decided. He has come to a manger in a poor backwater town to meet a family of traveling peasants. He is surrounded by the stench of animals and shepherds. And here he encounters the very God of the universe, who makes sense of all his anxiety and uncertainty. How beautiful would that nativity scene have been?

Faithful presence is what God asks of us in impossible situations. When we find life in God, when we put the source of zoe first and allow God to order our psyche, God transforms us into fountains of life. In a world of difficult choices, God does not demand that we have all the right answers. Rather we follow the example of Jesus by wading into the midst of the mess and waiting for God. We face our neighbors with love and joy and peace. We trust the Spirit to create in us patience, kindness, and generosity. We practice faithfulness, gentleness, and self-control. God's life flows through us into the world around us. To do otherwise puts us on the wrong side of the Christmas story.

9

HERODIAS

An opportunity came when Herod on his birthday gave a banquet for his courtiers and officers and for the leaders of Galilee. When his daughter [Salome] came in and danced, she pleased Herod and his guests; and the king said to the girl, "Ask me for whatever you wish, and I will give it." And he solemnly swore to her, "Whatever you ask me, I will give you, even half of my kingdom." She went out and said to her mother, "What should I ask for?" [Herodias] replied, "The head of John the baptizer." Immediately she rushed back to the king and requested, "I want you to give me at once the head of John the Baptist on a platter."

MARK 6:21-25

Herodias descended the dank stairwell, careful not to touch the walls. In the dim light of her torch, her eyes scanned the steps, alert for loose rock on which she might turn an ankle. She walked slowly to ensure the slave following her could see as well. He mustn't drop the meal.

As she reached the dungeon, she saw the prophet, his hunched form against the far wall. The form shifted at the sound of her approaching footsteps. The flame of her torch danced in the black pools of his eyes as he tried to discern the identity of his visitor.

Herodias secured the torch to a sconce on the back wall and settled onto the crude stool outside the cell. The slave stood behind her, holding an elaborate gold platter covered with a matching domed lid.

Herodias saw the prophet's eyes narrow as they adjusted to the light. Something flickered in them—not recognition, though he doubtless had discerned who she was. How many women had access to the prison? Perhaps it was contempt. Or indignation. No matter. She offered the prisoner a cold smile and said, "I thought it was time we met, John, son of Zechariah, called the Baptizer. I am Herodias, your queen."

The Baptizer watched her for a long moment. "Forgive me, Highness." His gravelly voice was thick with irony. "I am unschooled in the ways of the nobility. I was unaware the wife of a prince is still called a queen."

Herodias's grin didn't slip. "They say you're fearless, Baptizer. I am glad to see you live up to your reputation. It is, in fact, my marriage I came to discuss with you today. I am quite sure we can reach an understanding between the two of us that will see you back drowning people in the river in no time."

The Baptizer shifted. "Have you come to repent, to make ready the path of the Lord?" He made a show of searching the dungeon. "I am somewhat short on water, but if Her Majesty will summon a bath, we can make do."

Herodias arched her eyebrows. "And what will your followers think when they hear you asked to bathe with a queen?"

The prophet sputtered, trying for a retort, but Herodias laughed melodically. "John, no one wants you in this cell. It looks bad for Antipas to arrest a prophet of the Lord—almost as bad as having that prophet traipsing about his land, announcing to anyone who will listen that his marriage is an abomination."

She withdrew a key from the folds of her cloak, and her tone hardened. "You can walk out of here right now. Simply give me your word that no one—not Antipas nor I nor any of your acolytes—and not even the weeds in that desert you call home—will hear another word about our marriage from your lips."

The prophet did not move from his slouched position against the wall, but his voice was strong and clear. "The day of the Lord is at hand, Your Highness." He had turned her title into a barb. "His great wrath will fall upon all who are unfaithful—even his own chosen people. Now is the time to repent."

Herodias rolled her eyes. "Yes, yes, Baptizer. You're anxious to get back to preparing the Lord's way. So do we have a deal?"

The Baptizer's eyes lit with fanatical zeal. He continued as though she had not spoken. "But how can the people repent when their shepherds persist in sin? When a man steals his brother's wife, it is an abomination, whether that man is common or a king—or even a tetrarch." He threw the title at Herodias like a dagger.

Herodias sighed. "I suspected you would prove unwilling to see reason. Compromise has always been difficult for your kind. But I am not unreasonable. I trust some time as our guest will help you see that we need not be enemies." Herodias snapped her fingers, and the slave set the platter just outside the bars of the cell, then retreated to retrieve the torch.

Herodias stood. "Compliments of Antipas's personal cook. Possibly more enjoyable than your usual fare." With that, she turned and left the dungeon, abandoning the Baptizer to darkness.

Herodias descended the dank stairwell more quickly alone. She placed the torch back in the sconce and again sat on the crude stool. She noted the serving dish, still covered. She frowned. "Was the food not to your liking?"

The Baptizer had shifted toward her but now settled back against the wall. He held her gaze, but said nothing. Herodias sighed. "I had hoped you would branch out a bit. I'll see about getting something that meets your approval. You are, after all, a prophet of the Lord. So let us speak, you and I. Let us come to an agreement with which we can both live."

John glared at her. "We will not speak. You are unaccompanied. You do not even wear a veil. I am a man of God."

A surprised laugh escaped Herodias's lips. "You fear I'll tempt you, Baptizer?" She ran her hands suggestively over her body and laughed again. "Perhaps I'll steal you from God the way I stole Antipas from his Nabatean wife?" She spit on the ground. "I am no whore. You'd do well to remember that when you are freed."

The Baptizer remained silent. Was it only the torchlight, or did hope flicker in his eyes?

"I was not completely honest before, Baptizer." She made her tone warm with a trace of vulnerability. "I am not here for myself. I am here for my daughter, Salome." She looked away for a moment, and when she held his gaze again, her eyes glistened. "You don't have children, do you? No time to marry while you play the Lord's mistress." Her wry tone stole the barb from the jest. "Perhaps you don't understand. But if you do not trust me, then trust Solomon. Was it not he who said, 'Sons are a heritage from the Lord, the fruit of the womb a reward'? Salome is my heritage, my reward from the Lord. I will do anything to give her happiness and peace."

Pride swelled in Herodias's chest. "My daughter is beautiful—more beautiful even than I was. And she inherited her father's lack of guile. I have tried to impart to her even a scrap of cunning, but Salome simply does not have the mind for politics. Were her father a person of any note, it wouldn't matter. But he is a forgotten prince of a speck of land that matters only because it's between two empires. Even with Augustus's influence, the best she could hope for is to be given to the lackey of some client king.

"I will have better than that for my daughter. At least she could remain among her own people. But her only hope was Antipas, who was already married, and Philip. And neither gained anything from marrying the daughter of Herod II, Herod the Great's forgotten son."

The prophet's dark form remained unmoved.

"Do you know what it is to be a Herodian, Baptizer? To be a pawn shuffled about at the whims of a grandfather who doted on you even as he executed your father? To be made the princess of Israel, only to have it stripped away?"

Herodias became almost wistful as she thought about her former husband. "You've not met Herod II, Baptizer, but you would love him. He is earnest and simple. Doubtless if he had been named tetrarch of the Galilee, or even king of the Jews as he once was promised, he would have named you high prophet of the royal court by now."

Herodias's eyes, seeing distant memories, suddenly focused again on John. "His kindness is his daughter's undoing. He did not know how to provide a suitable marriage for Salome. But I can. I will not see my daughter shuffled about at the whims of foreign kings. She will have better than I did. Antipas will ensure she is married to Philip. She will live among her own people."

The Baptizer remained silent, though his eyes never left Herodias's. She searched his eyes for a sign of compassion but found only righteous condemnation. So she shifted her tactics. "Give me your word that you will no longer mention our marriage, and Antipas and I will receive your baptism."

Shock registered on John's face as he straightened. "What?"

"At your word, I will release you. Antipas and I will accompany you to the Jordan. We will submit to your baptism of repentance. And you will return to your ministry, the whole country knowing you have the ear of Antipas. Perhaps Philip will even follow suit. You get a nation that is returning to God, and my daughter marries Philip."

A long silence followed, and John finally spoke. "Fools think their own way is right, but the wise listen to advice."

Herodias barked a short laugh and said in disbelief, "You quote Solomon to lecture me on marriage? Who is the fool here, Baptizer?" Her voice was an iron dagger. "I will have your silence. Marrying Antipas was difficult enough without you telling anyone who would listen we were incurring the Lord's wrath. I tried everything to get him to shut your mouth. Begging. Threatening. Asking very nicely. Finally shaming worked. 'You're the ruler of the Galilee. The son of Herod the Great. This worm cannot speak of you so!' Even then, he would not kill you. Only arrest you, throw you in here."

Herodias laughed again. "Had he only known how afraid you are of women. We could simply have invited you to dinner to silence you."

The Baptizer growled. "I do not fear you. I fear the Lord God."

Herodias rolled her eyes. "If the Lord is angry that this mother seeks to do better by her daughter, let him come tell me himself. He at least is not afraid to speak to a woman. Did he not speak to Deborah, to Hannah?"

With that, she departed, leaving the prophet in darkness and silence.

Herodias descended the stairwell, leading two men covered with the dust of the road. As they gained the floor of the dungeon, she called out, "Baptizer, your disciples have returned." She noted that a slave had removed the serving dish.

John climbed to his feet and pressed against the bars of the cell. Again Herodias placed the torch in the sconce, but this time she retreated to allow the disciples to crowd close to their master. They offered him water from a skin they had brought and some bread and honey, which he ate greedily. As he ate, the two disciples shifted nervously.

As soon as the Baptizer had finished his meager meal, he demanded, "What did Jesus say?"

One of the men said, "We asked as you commanded. 'Are you the one who is to come, or are we to wait for another?'" He paused, swallowed.

"Yes, yes. What did he say?"

"Go and tell John what you have seen and heard: the blind receive their sight, the lame walk, the lepers are cleansed, the deaf hear, the dead are raised, the poor have good news brought to them."

Herodias recognized Isaiah's words.

John flinched as though struck. Clearly he recognized them as well. "What else? What else did he say?"

The men exchanged another glance. "'Blessed—blessed is anyone who takes no offense at me.' That's all, teacher. I'm sorry."

Herodias watched as the men prayed together. After some time, the disciples made to leave. They turned to her, obviously unsure how to proceed.

"You may leave," she said. "You know the way out."

The men turned back to John, who had already sunk to the floor. He waved them away. "Leave us." So dismissed, the men left quickly, stealing furtive glances back at the queen and the prophet.

Once they were gone, Herodias returned to the stool. The Baptizer didn't meet her gaze, and she realized he was weeping softly. "Jesus," she said. "You sent word to Jesus of Nazareth. Your cousin."

The Baptizer's damp eyes found hers, and he saw surprise and a little fear in them.

She said, "You didn't think we would discover the connection? I told you, prophet, Antipas is infatuated with you." A kind grin curled the corner of her mouth. "A lesser woman might be jealous.

"He met your father once, did you know that? It was not long after you were born. Antipas was the crown prince, and the magicians of Parthia had declared their intentions to discover the newborn Messiah. I'm sure you know the story, how Grandfather ordered the boys of Bethlehem slaughtered."

The Baptizer turned toward her. He had not heard that story.

"Antipas remembers your father because he was so sure the magicians had it right. He boasted to the whole council about you, born as a herald of the Messiah."

At the mention of his father's pride, a tear escaped the Baptizer's eye and traced a stream down his cheek.

"Grandfather didn't much care for messiahs, prophets, or magicians. But Antipas was always more pious. When you began preaching out in the wilderness, as you gained followers, it didn't take him long to put two and two together. John, son of Zechariah. John, preparing the way of the Lord, offering a baptism of repentance. How many of you could there possibly be? And if Antipas could discover who your father was, how much easier do you think it was to determine that you and this Jesus of Nazareth are cousins?"

Herodias smiled. "Are you truly the cousin of God's anointed, John? The blood of God's anointed flows in *my* veins, you know. Not all of Herod's wives were Hasmonean, but my grandmother was. I am a descendant of Judas Maccabeus—the very man whom God anointed to drive out the pagans who desecrated his holy temple.

"Is this our lot—to be related to greatness but not great ourselves? Are we puppets the Almighty uses to glorify those he truly loves?"

The Baptizer glowered. "Do not mock God's anointed."

"It is not Jesus I mock, Baptizer." Herodias struggled to keep the contempt from her voice. "You are kin to the Messiah, but you yourself are not anointed, are you? No, of course you're not. Like Antipas, you're from the wrong half of the family. Everyone knows your speech. The one who comes *after* you is God's anointed. You're not fit to—how did it go? Lick his sandal?"

Herodias breathed deeply, then spoke again. "How different the two of you are. You eat insects, you wear sackcloth, you play Elijah in the wilderness. But your cousin travels the land, feasting and preaching. I hear they call him the friend of sinners. How that must grate on your righteous sensibilities. Is it true that he travels with women, that he teaches them? If he were in this cell and not you, would he speak freely with me?"

The Baptizer couldn't restrain himself. "My cousin keeps his own counsel."

Herodias saw she had found a wound. She pressed carefully. "If your cousin is indeed the promised Messiah, why does he not come to your aid? That's what you asked him, isn't it?"

The Baptizer looked down at the floor of his cell. Herodias continued. "'The Spirit of the Lord is upon me, because he has anointed me to bring good news to the poor.'" She smiled when John's wide eyes met hers again. "Of course I know Isaiah. Do not think that because I don't share your zealotry I know nothing, son of Zechariah. I know how the rest of the proclamation goes too.

'He has sent me to proclaim release to the captives.' No jubilee year is complete without the release of prisoners."

Herodias's voice held not a trace of laughter anymore. "I had heard Jesus' tongue was as sharp as yours, but this is cruel. Your cousin has been trumpeting Isaiah's mission as his own, reading that prophecy in every village across the countryside. So why does he not free you? Why answer you with Isaiah's words but omit that promise? And then to insist you not take offense—Jesus may as well have told you to rot in prison. Why? He's made it clear he has no great love for Antipas either. So why abandon you here?"

A new appreciation for her intelligence flashed in John's eyes, but his pain overshadowed it.

Herodias saw that pain. "I did not think I could ever pity you, Baptizer, but I must say you are in a desperate place. You have been abandoned even by the one for whom you prepared the way—one who is your very own flesh and blood.

"I had not intended to make this offer again. But your lord and your messiah has abandoned you. So will you keep silent on my union with Antipas? Your cousin does not feel the need to mention our marriage in his preaching. Why should you? If he won't save you, at least follow his lead and save yourself. Give your word, and you walk free right now. I'll send men after your disciples."

John looked away, and Herodias saw the strain in his shoulders. She knew the look of a man at the end of his hope. Had she pressed too hard? The moments drained away. Finally Herodias stood. "Well, Baptizer? Will you keep silent for my family, since yours will not speak for you?"

The prophet turned again to her, eyes aflame once more. He began to quote Job: "See, he will kill me. I have no hope; but I will defend my ways to his face. This will be my salvation: that the *godless*"—he spat the word at her—"shall not come before him."

Herodias sighed deeply and stood to reclaim the torch. "For your own sake, Baptizer, I hope you truly are as righteous as was Job."

With that, she departed, leaving the prophet in darkness and silence.

Herodias descended the stairwell, surefooted but slow. Again a slave followed, bearing a platter. From within the dish came a steady, faint buzzing, punctuated by occasional thumps of something striking the inside of the lid. The queen once more placed the torch on the wall and once more sat on her stool. She frowned and wondered when she had started thinking that stool was hers. The Baptizer stared at her, his mouth set in a perpetual frown, eyes curious and defiant.

"I think I finally understand why you have taken such a special interest in my marriage, prophet. The people think you're Elijah—the great prophet of Israel returned to announce God's coming judgment. No mystery whether you agree. Was it you or your father who chose the costume and sticking to the diet? All very impressive." As if to punctuate her observation, something thumped loudly against the inside of the dish behind her.

"Of course, if you're Elijah, we know who I am. What would the hero of Israel be without his Jezebel? How fortunate for you that I seduced Antipas away from his wife! How fortunate for you my whoredoms are so literal!"

The Baptizer glowered at her. "Sin never brings fortune for God's people."

Herodias spat. "Sin, you say. I build no temples to Baal! I establish no sacred poles for Astarte! I worship the God of my fathers and yours. If I am guilty of anything, it is refusing to consign my daughter to a life decided by the whims of another."

Weary as he was, John's voice was strong with indignation. "No man is lost who submits himself to the will of God."

"No man?" Herodias leaned in. "Your fortune, Baptizer, is to have been born a man. Do you think the crowds would have come from Jerusalem to bathe in your river if you were a Miriam or a Jael? When you call me a whore, when you decry my marriage as an affront to the Lord, are you sure they listen to you because you are righteous and not because I am a woman?"

The Baptizer remained silent. Herodias let the question linger unanswered in the air, the continuous buzz from the platter accompanying her words.

Finally she continued. "You know I was raised in Rome, in Augustus's own house. I was raised under the watchful eye of Livia Drusilla, wife of the emperor of Rome. How to describe her to you, Baptizer? Now that she has died, she will certainly be elevated to divinity, and rightly so. She was as one of the great statues of Rome. Beautiful in the way Roman women are beautiful. Utterly composed and controlled. She was the ideal wife for the emperor. Chaste, faithful, powerful."

A guttural scoffing sound slipped from the Baptizer's mouth. "Apparently she was a poor teacher."

Herodias smiled thinly. "You think because I divorced Herod II, I am nothing like bold, faithful Livia Drusilla? How provincial you are, Baptizer. Once Augustus had ascended to the throne of Rome, Livia conspired with him to take her as his wife. She divorced her husband and married herself to Augustus. Some insist Livia was little more than a casualty of Augustus's maneuvers to control Rome. But those who say such things have never stood in the presence of Livia Drusilla. She was Augustus's equal in every way.

They were two voices singing in perfect harmony. Augustus loved her, doted on her. He gave her lands; she conducted her own business and led negotiations. None should a *proper* Roman woman do. But she was Livia Drusilla, wife of the First Citizen. She did as she pleased."

The Baptizer growled. "Pride goes before destruction, and a haughty spirit before a fall. It is—"

"Save your condemnation, Baptizer. You denounce as pride what you should recognize as love. Have I not told you that I act not for myself, but for Salome? My daughter is everything to me. Livia knew what awaited Salome if we did not leave Rome. It was she who hit upon the solution. She had met Antipas when he came to Rome after Grandfather's death, when he was named tetrarch. She was impressed by his demeanor, by his audacity, by his will. And she saw by the way he looked at me that his passions are his flaw.

"It was no difficult matter to seduce Antipas away from his Nabatean wife. She is a great, dumb behemoth; I have no doubt that conversation with her is nearly as stimulating as talking with you. Men's passions are easily inflamed; Antipas was captivated. The next morning, I had little trouble convincing him that a union with me made for a stronger nation—and a more enjoyable life.

"There will be a feast this month in honor of Antipas's birthday. At the conclusion of the feast, we will announce that Salome has been engaged to Philip. My daughter will be as much a queen as am I. She will be among her people. Philip is a good man—a touch too prideful, but such will not trouble Salome.

"Hear me, Baptizer. I will see my daughter married to Philip."

John shrugged. "I care not who your daughter marries, so long as she remains righteous."

Herodias stood. "You have discovered the limits of my mercy. I am not interested in your judgment of my union with Antipas. I am not interested in your baptism or this messiah who has abandoned you. I am interested only in your compliance. Antipas is convinced your continued disapproval of our marriage will scare Philip off. Antipas has always concerned himself too much with what the common folk think—he is his father in that regard. But I do not share his concern.

"We can kill you and you will become a martyr—or you would have if your cousin were not out preaching your message. Some of your disciples will lose faith, but most will simply join his cause. My husband is wrong. You are no longer relevant, Baptizer. The way has been prepared. God is finished with you, and no chariot comes to take you to heaven.

"So I will give you one final chance. Your word sets you free. But if you refuse me tonight, rest assured that you will not live out the month. So may the Lord do to me and more also if I do not fulfill my word. I have enjoyed our talks, but my affection for your grumbling pales in comparison to my love for my daughter. Save your speeches. Save your condemnation. Save your zeal and judgment for someone who would listen. I will not. I want to hear from you only that you will agree, if not for your own sake then for my daughter's."

In response, the Baptizer finished quoting his proverb: "It is better to be of a lowly spirit among the poor than to divide the spoil with the proud."

"As you will." Herodias stood. Antipas's feast was fast approaching, and she had much to prepare. As she retrieved the torch from the sconce, another thump came from the serving platter. The torchlight gleamed off the lid.

Herodias spared one final glance at John, who had slouched against the dungeon wall. "You will no doubt find this recipe more to your liking. Our cook struggled with the ingredients; locusts are notoriously difficult to herd. Consider this your last meal."

Herodias climbed from the dungeon, leaving the prophet in darkness and silence.

10

THE CAT'S IN THE CRADLE

The Fingerprints Our Families Leave on Us

I'm not the only person who has awkward Thanksgiving family memories, right? Growing up, Thanksgiving always meant a family reunion on my dad's side. My grandfather, his siblings, and all their descendants gathered annually at the Methodist church my dad grew up in, the church his grandfather pastored for several years. At least three of those long wooden tables that populate the closets of every church building in America were laid out in the fellowship hall. (Where else?) The tables were filled to overflowing, and sliced turkey and pans of sweet potatoes were brought from the nearby kitchen whenever they ran low. It was our annual chance to see cousins, second cousins, great-uncles, and aunts who were otherwise scattered across the Midwest.

The highlight of the day was always the tackle football game played between lunch and dinner. No one knows who began this tradition or why that person thought the best time for grown men to slam into and grapple one another was between large feasts. Nevertheless, somewhere around two, all the men who were old enough to play and too young to know better gathered in the field behind the church building to play football.

By the time I was in college, the reunion had shrunk, as reunions do. The football games had gotten quite a bit smaller too.

At this particularly awkward Thanksgiving memory, eight of us took the field. I linked up with my uncle Craig and a couple of cousins against my father, younger brother, and more cousins.

My brother was in high school at the time and a star of his school's football team. He had recently reached the point where he could beat me in wrestling matches (he took third in the state of Kansas his senior year) and ran significantly faster than I. So I took great joy in one play where I stopped him on a fourth down. It's possible I took a little *too* much joy; the level of peacocking and trash talk was what most would consider excessive.

My father decided to teach me a lesson and squared off against me on the next play. Whether I was in the fabled "zone" that day or just got lucky, I scored a touchdown. And because I am the epitome of a good winner, I doubled down on both the peacocking and the trash talk. I wasn't playing anymore. I wanted to win, to be the best. I turned the game into something ugly, and everyone could tell. The football game ended shortly after that, and Thanksgiving dinner was much more awkward than usual—at least for me.

Around this same time in my life, I began to realize the men in my family have a problem: we're stubborn. That's not exactly the most grotesque skeleton anyone's ever found in a closet, and we certainly didn't invent stubbornness. But if there is a sin that marks the men of my family, it's this particular brand of pride.

My father told me stories when I was young about the conflicts he and his father had. And I've seen the same stubborn sense of self-righteousness in me as I saw in them. My brother and I often compare notes on how that pride affects every area of our lives—our families, our work, our friendships.

Our families inescapably shape us. Maybe like me you are a child of divorce and grew up in single-parent homes, shuffling between blended families. Or you lost a parent. Maybe you're adopted or grew up in foster care. Or maybe you grew up in a nuclear family one white picket fence away from Ward and June Cleaver. However we grew up, those environments and those families left a mark on us. How good or bad those marks are depends on the particular environment, of course, but no family is perfect (apologies to the Cleavers).

Herodias was shaped by the family that raised her, and the Herodians were no Cleavers.

Wicked Queen 2.0

It would be easy to blame Herodias's sins on her grandfather, Herod the Great. If she were alive today, Herodias would be the star of *Keeping Up with the Herodians*, and YouTube would be flooded with videos of her complaining about her terrible childhood, her loser ex-husband, and her difficult life.

We know very little about Herodias from the Bible. Mark tells us that Herod Antipas arrested John the Baptizer because John openly criticized Antipas's marriage to Herodias.[1] Antipas had been married to a princess from the Nabatean kingdom, a client kingdom of Rome that had given the Herodians trouble for decades. Antipas's marriage represented an uneasy peace, one that his divorce disrupted.[2]

John the Baptizer wasn't concerned with the politics, however. He criticized the divorce as immoral, an affront to God. John's repeated vocal criticism of Herod Antipas for this divorce and remarriage is why Antipas arrested John.

Despite Antipas's anger at John, Mark tells us Antipas was afraid to kill the prophet. Mark implied that Herodias hated John so much that Antipas had to protect him from her. And Mark tells us that Herodias conspired against Antipas to see John dead.[3]

Many Jews of Jesus' day anticipated Elijah's return ahead of the Messiah, and Mark positioned John as Elijah returned. He would come as a harbinger of the end. As he did the first time, Elijah would call God's people to repent.

Not only did Mark introduce John with a prophecy from Isaiah, but John also dressed as Elijah did (in a simple camel-skin garment) and maintained a similar diet (locusts and honey). Elijah spent a lot of time across the Jordan River, the traditional boundary of the Promised Land, and John called people to the Jordan to be baptized. They symbolically returned to the wilderness, repented, and entered back into the Promised Land as God's people, washed and ready to welcome the Messiah.

Conveniently for Mark's narrative, John came with his own archenemies. Just as Ahab and Jezebel opposed Elijah, so John faced Antipas and Herodias. Just as Elijah condemned Ahab's marriage to Jezebel, John condemned Antipas's marriage to Herodias. But Herodias was more than just a warmed-over Jezebel.

Because Herodias is absent from the rest of the Scriptures, we must rely on nonbiblical sources to tell us what Herodias was like. Those sources make it difficult not to feel bad for Herodias. She grew up in a mixture of privilege and terror. She lived in the center of the Roman Empire, but as a foreigner. She was royalty, but the granddaughter of a vassal king. She was a woman. She lived in the center of power with enough privilege to *see* power, but she had no power herself. Many of the slaves in Augustus's household had more influence than she did.

Herodias grew up far from the court of her grandfather, Herod. But while Herod ruled thousands of miles from her, he shaped the course of her life. Herod and his second wife, Mariamne I, gave birth to Aristobulus IV, who married his cousin, Berenice.[4] They had three sons and two daughters, one of whom was Herodias. Because of Herod's close relationship with Augustus, Aristobulus and his brother were educated in Rome, in Augustus's own house, which means Herodias grew up in the very center of the Roman Empire, under the guidance of Augustus and his wife, Livia.

Herodias was also a child bride, married off to her uncle. While we rightly condemn both child marriage and incest today, both were common in the ancient world, particularly among royal families. Herodias's first wedding to her uncle, Herod II, would have raised no eyebrows. Even John the Baptizer didn't condemn that union.

Incestuous marriage is only the tip of the iceberg for Herodias. Here are some highlights of the Herodian family history that pertain especially to her. Imagine how much fun *their* family reunions were:

- Herodias's great-aunt Salome I manipulated her grandfather, Herod, into killing Herodias's grandmother, Mariamne I, more than a decade before Herodias was born.
- That great-aunt was also Herodias's grandmother, since Salome I's daughter, Berenice, was Herodias's mother.
- Herodias's father, Aristobulus, was by all accounts very good-looking and wildly popular among the Jews. That popularity made his father, Herod, very nervous. Herod's oldest son, Antipater II, used that jealousy to convince Herod that his handsome younger brother was conspiring against them both, so Herod killed Herodias's father when she was only eight years old.
- After her father was executed, Herod decided his granddaughter, Herodias, should be married to her uncle, Herod II, who was second in line for the throne, after her uncle Antipater II (the one who had her father killed). Herod engaged Antipater II to Herodias's older sister.

- Antipater II (the uncle who got her father, Aristobulus, killed by convincing Herod that Aristobulus wanted to kill him) actually did try to kill Herod a couple of years later. Herod executed him.
- Herodias's husband, Herod II, should have been next in line for the throne, but because his mother (Herod's third wife) knew about the assassination plot, Herod removed Herodias's husband, Herod II, from the line of succession.[5]
- Herod named Archelaus, the eldest son of his fourth wife, his new heir.
- Herod II and Herodias had a daughter. Her name was either Herodias, after her mother, or Salome, after her great-grandmother. Given the Herodian proclivity for naming themselves Herod, there's no way to know. Most scholars call the daughter Salome to avoid confusion—at least a little.
- After her grandfather died, Herodias's uncles all traveled to Rome to argue before Augustus over who got to be king. Augustus divided the kingdom into quarters, giving half to Archelaus, a quarter to Herod Antipas, and a quarter to Philip.[6]
- Herod Archelaus proved to be worse than his father. He was deposed after a decade for being terrible, and his territory was converted into the Roman province of Judea, complete with a Roman governor.[7]
- At some point after Antipas became tetrarch over the Galilee, he divorced his Nabatean wife to marry Herodias.
- After Antipas and Herodias married, her daughter, Salome, married her uncle/brother-in-law Philip the Tetrarch.

Exhausted yet? Keeping track of Herodias's family tree is more daunting than tracing houses in *Game of Thrones* or sorting out

Henry VIII's wives. What we know of Herodias comes to us because her story weaves in among the stories of the Herodian kings and tetrarchs. She was born to, engaged to, married to, divorced from. Herodias is mentioned in the Bible only because of her divorce and remarriage.

Herodias was born to a family of schemers and plotters, a family for whom power and security must be achieved at all costs. Family was never a safe space for Herodias. Parents and grandparents were killed. Uncles were prospective husbands or would-be assassins. Mothers, sisters, and cousins were swapped routinely to serve the interests of whichever man was currently in the line of succession. Herodias grew to womanhood knowing her family as the people who manipulated her to get what they wanted.

Another family shaped Herodias, a family whose influence makes the portrait of her we see in Mark all the more probable. Herod sent his sons by Mariamne I to be educated in Augustus's house in Rome. Herodias was born and raised in the household of Caesar Augustus, under the guidance of his wife, Livia. Though Herodias was a Jew, she was raised Roman, and Roman women held a different place in society than Jewish women did, especially among the nobility. Livia was widely regarded as Augustus's equal and became (in)famous for the masculine ways she employed power. Though the traditional Roman woman's place was to oversee the home, Livia traveled with Augustus. She greeted dignitaries and participated in ceremonial diplomatic duties. She even mediated between Augustus and Roman citizens.[8]

So Herodias grew to womanhood watching a strong royal woman exercise her will freely, in partnership with the emperor of Rome. And Mark's Herodias is a cunning, vengeful woman who saw John as an obstacle to her power and position. When her husband would not execute him, Herodias took matters into her own hands, crafting a clever scheme that neither Antipas nor John saw coming. In a few brief verses, Herodias demonstrated the ruthlessness of her grandfather Herod and the political savvy of her patroness Livia. She was the product of her families.

Mark positioned Herodias as a latter-day Jezebel who opposed God's divinely ordained prophet because she was evil. But as with Jezebel, the shortcomings of the evil-queen trope don't let Herodias be fully human. She was a daughter, a sister, a wife, a mother.

Herod's and Livia's legacies shaped Herodias. She learned from the time she was born that the only power, the only agency she would have was what she took for herself. As a queen, she would command no armies. As a Jew, she would occupy no Senate seat. As a woman, she could silence no opposition. The tools available to her were cunning and persuasion, and she grew up in a family where those were wielded as dangerous weapons.

How could Herodias possibly have seen John as anything other than an opponent? And given how both Herod and Livia treated their opponents, how else would Herodias have responded to someone who was a threat to her power?

None of this excuses Herodias. No matter how our families shape us, we are accountable for our actions. But perhaps her story should give us pause. Her family shaped her so that it was very difficult for her to hear God's voice calling her to repentance through John. Instead, like Cain, she lashed out, killing the voice of challenge rather than heeding the prophet.

The Apple Doesn't Fall Far

Every family has its own unique legacies of sin. In the Scriptures, we clearly see generational sin, and God warns us against it as early as the Exodus story, when Israel receives the Ten Commandments.

Woven into the commandment against idolatry is this: "I the Lord your God am a jealous God, punishing children for the iniquity of parents, to the third and the fourth generation of those who reject me, but showing steadfast love to the thousandth generation of those who love me and keep my commandments" (Exodus 20:5-6).

When I was a teenager, these verses terrified me. My parents divorced when I was thirteen, and I spent a lot of years wondering exactly how God would punish me (and even, possibly, my great-grandchildren) for what my parents had done. In recent years, I've learned I'm descended from a slave owner in Virginia. I'll never know the extent to which my ancestors are to blame for the state of race relations in the United States today. It's impossible to determine how much of the good I enjoy is possible because at some point in the past, a member of my family owned other human beings. But the reality is that in both recent and distant history, my family has sinned.

I grew up in a church tradition that never examined sin as anything other than morally wrong actions committed by an individual. When I did something wrong, I often imagined a giant chalkboard in heaven where God would add another hash mark beside my name.[9]

In this understanding of sin, the concept of generational sin seems profoundly unjust. Why should I suffer because my parents chose to divorce? Why should I be punished because an ancestor of mine bought and sold other humans? Why should I bear the consequences of anything someone else did? Even small children know that's not right.

The problem is that experience tells us sin *does* get passed down from generation to generation. Children of alcoholics are much more likely to become alcoholics themselves. Victims of sexual abuse are up to three times more likely to become sexual abusers themselves.[10] From our families, we learn to fight and we learn how to perceive our bodies. The critical voice in our head sounds like an older sibling, a parent, a grandparent, an aunt, or an uncle. Go back enough generations, and certain sins pop up over and over again. Like a tree that grows around a fence, our family trees become entwined with certain sins.

We certainly can speak of sin as individual bad actions. But the Bible speaks of sin as much larger and more insidious than merely individual action. Catholic theologian Robert Barron describes it as an atmosphere that poisons us from the moment we're born:

> There is no moral act or psychological attitude that does not, in one sense, affect the entire organism which is the human race, and there is therefore no warping or misuse of spiritual energy that does not adversely affect the whole "body" of the humanum. The abuse of freedom, from the earliest people down through the centuries, has set up a sort of negative field of force that, willy-nilly, affects every person on the planet today. Egotism exists as a kind of poisonous spiritual atmosphere that all of us breathe from the moment we enter into the human condition. The originating sin of fear moves into our institutions, our governments, our modes of social organization, our systems of education, our languages, our religions, our literature and philosophy, our mythic stories, our military establishments, our styles of recreation, our economic structures. Through these systems and institutions, sin surrounds us, envelops us, almost determines us. Like the prisoners in Plato's cave, we find ourselves—despite our best efforts and intentions—held in place by the shackles of institutionalized sin.[11]

Sin is inescapable because we have been pumping it into our institutions, cultures, and families since humans have walked the earth. Sin, like a disease, infects us from the first breath we take, warping us as we grow. We shrug and say, "To err is human." We have normalized sin to the point that we can't even see that it *is* sin anymore.

How could Christians have marched in the Crusades? How could Christians have actively participated in every level of the slave trade? How could Christians murder people they consider heretics? How could Christians turn a blind eye to the Holocaust? Today we make excuses: "They were people of their time. It's not fair to judge the actions of yesterday by the morality of today."

Fine (I guess). But the more important question here is: How am I a "person of my time"? What sins might I be participating in today—totally assured of my own righteousness—that will be condemned by the church of the future? Might they ask, "How could Christians have spewed hatred and death threats at the LGBTQ community? Why was the church so segregated? How could the Western church ignore the millions in the Global South who don't have access to clean water? Didn't they realize that creation is a precious gift from our Creator? How could they have been so careless with their food, their fuel, and their trash?"[12] Sin has thoroughly warped the very fabric of our institutions. Like fish that cannot comprehend the ocean, we are blind to sin because it's so pervasive, because it's been infecting us since the moment of our birth.

We inherit sin from our families, from our culture, from our world. We grow up warped and twisted. Our idolatry has disastrous consequences, not just for us, but also for the generations that follow us.

Somewhere I Belong

Camp conversion syndrome helped me to understand the problem of generational sin. I grew up in a church with a large, active youth group. We went to summer camp every year, so I was familiar with the "camp conversion" phenomenon. Camp conversion syndrome happens when a teenager has an experience at camp—either a conversion or rededication of his life to God. He makes any number of commitments, swearing off anything from dating to drugs and alcohol to swearing. And for about two weeks after camp, he sticks to those commitments. But sooner or later (usually sooner), the teen has reverted to his pre-camp behaviors.

We could dedicate a whole book to problematizing the camp conversion experience—harping on the emotionalism of altar calls and the dangers of tying a relationship with God so closely to behaviors. But in my six years as a youth pastor, I saw plenty of kids experience genuine movements of the Spirit at camps (and retreats and so on). I witnessed genuine changes and earnest desires to follow God's way and share in the life of the Spirit.

And then those same kids went home, back into the environments in which they had learned sin in the first place. The problem wasn't that the teens hadn't experienced genuine change. They had. They had shown up as a square peg, and God had transformed them to a round peg. But when they returned home, to their families, to school, to their friends, they found nothing else had changed. A square hole was still waiting for them.

In my experience, it took about two weeks of not fitting for most kids to decide it was easier to go back to acting like a square peg. It wasn't that their experience wasn't real. It was that the pull of their sinful family structures was so strong.

Sin is more than the sum of our immoral actions. Sin is a toxic atmosphere we've been breathing in since birth. That said, being born into patterns of sin is not the same as sinning. In the wake of the exile, many Israelites wondered why they had to bear the punishment for their parents' sins. Israel's prophets had long warned that if Israel did not turn from idolatry to worship God, God would give them over to their enemies. They didn't listen, so God followed through. Without God's protection and provision, the Babylonian Empire conquered Judea, destroyed Jerusalem and the temple, and deported the Jewish leaders to Babylon.

The Israelites understood the exile as the consequence of their sin. But the exile didn't affect only the adult Israelites. Their children bore the weight of exile too. When they turned to the Scripture to understand why, they found that same promise in the Ten Commandments. They protested as we do, "It's not fair!"

To their protest, Ezekiel announced,

> You say, "Why should not the son suffer for the iniquity of the father?" When the son has done what is lawful and right, and has been careful to observe all my statutes, he shall surely live. The person who sins shall die. A child shall not suffer for the iniquity of a parent, nor a parent suffer for the iniquity of a child; the righteousness of the righteous shall be his own, and the wickedness of the wicked shall be his own. (Ezekiel 18:19-20)

God promises that only the person who sins is accountable for that sin. The person who follows the way of God will share in God's life. This is very good news at the individual level: we are not held accountable for the sins of our parents (or their parents or their great-grandparents, and so on).

But there is a gray area: while we are not held accountable for the sin we're born into, that sin corrupts us. This atmosphere of sin warps us into beings for whom acting against God's will feels natural. The insidious truth of sin is that it convinces us we are less than we were created to be.

When we are saved, God makes us new creations. The Holy Spirit—the same Spirit that raised Jesus from the dead—makes us new. God enables us to live in the new reality that Jesus' resurrection inaugurated, what the Scriptures call the kingdom of God.

But we still live in that old world, corrupted by sin. Though we're given new lungs, we still breathe that old, poisoned air. If we're not diligent, we slide back into old patterns of sin without realizing it. Though we've been transformed into round pegs, we often find it easier to act like squares.

A Legacy of Life

My mother is a licensed family systems therapist. If you were to go to her for counseling, your whole first session would be spent drawing your family tree going back at least three generations and discussing how each person in the tree interacts with all the others. A significant component of the family systems therapist's job is helping you understand how the attitudes and behaviors that brought you to therapy have been produced and encouraged by the family system you're part of.

As you begin to heal, the therapist's job shifts to helping you prepare for how your family system will react to your healing, because our families are not typically happy when we begin to heal. Every system is conservative; it resists change. Healing is change, and whether we're healing from psychological trauma or we're being made new in Christ, the sinful systems that shaped us resist.

Left to our own power, we're all doomed to camp conversion syndrome. Fortunately, when the Spirit gives us new life, we are folded into the church, the body of Christ. Jesus tells us the church is a spiritual family, one that supersedes the families into which we were born.

> [Jesus'] mother and his brothers came; and standing outside, they sent to him and called him. A crowd was sitting around him; and they said to him, "Your mother and your brothers and sisters are outside, asking for you." And he replied, "Who are my mother and my brothers?" And looking at those who sat around him, he said, "Here are my mother and my brothers! Whoever does the will of God is my brother and sister and mother." (Mark 3:31-35)

If Jesus' words sound radical to you, they were even more so in the ancient world. But his words are good news for all of us who inherited sin from our families. Jesus invites us to follow him and to be reborn into a new family marked by the waters of baptism.

The church is a new spiritual family. It is a new spiritual culture. It is a new spiritual institution. The church is the kingdom of God, the new reality inaugurated by Jesus' resurrection, bursting forth in the midst of our sinful, broken institutions, cultures, and families. The church brings together people from every walk of life. People of every shape, size, age, and color. People formed in any number of sinful institutions, cultures, and families, but who have all been made new by the same Spirit who raised Jesus from the dead.

Together we learn how to be the people of God. We sing songs together that teach us the language of faith. We pray together. We read the Scriptures, exploring our new family heritage together. We approach the table and share in bread and wine that we might receive the grace to continue to work out our salvation together. We serve together, imitating the self-giving love of our king, the firstborn from among the dead.

Along the way, we begin to see ourselves reflected in the lives of our spiritual brothers and sisters. Attitudes and behaviors that we never gave a second thought suddenly seem strange, problematic, even sinful. We learn that blowing up isn't the only way to respond to conflict. We learn that we can share our thoughts without judgment. We learn how to love ourselves by experiencing the love of others. In the church, among the people of God, the Spirit grafts us into the body of Christ, into a new family, and we learn how to live into this new life Jesus has won for us.[13]

The good news is that generational sin isn't the end of the story. Even in Exodus, God promised, "But [I show] steadfast love to the thousandth generation of those who love me and keep my commandments" (20:6). Sin is not all we inherit from our parents. Both our spiritual and our biological families can form a strong legacy of faithfulness. Perhaps you learned from your parents a strong work ethic or a spirit of quiet, humble faithfulness. My parents taught me how to be welcoming and hospitable. They imparted to me a concern for outsiders that *they* inherited from *their* parents.

The faithfulness we learn from the church is inherited too. Go back in my genealogy far enough, and you'll find Michael Miksch, the man who brought the Moravian Brotherhood Church to North America. My great-grandfather, Paul Life, is the United Methodist pastor I mentioned at the beginning of the chapter. I grew up hearing stories of the churches he pastored, including the one where we had our Thanksgiving family reunion and another where he accepted the pulpit after the previous pastor ran off with a sixteen-year-old parishioner. There is story after story of how he brought hope and healing to people no one else thought were worth their time.

It's not so surprising, then, that I pastor a church for people who haven't found a place in traditional church settings. I come from a long line of people whose faith compelled them to the margins, to the disenchanted and disenfranchised. This legacy of faithfulness extends through my family tree for generation after generation.

None of us comes from a perfect family. But the Spirit, through Jesus, invites us all to join the family of God. We can learn to see our sin and cultivate new habits of faithfulness that will echo down through the generations and into the halls of eternity.

11

JUDAS

Judas Iscariot, who was one of the twelve, went to the chief priests in order to betray him to them. When they heard it, they were greatly pleased, and promised to give him money. So he began to look for an opportunity to betray him.

Mark 14:10-11

Tuesday Midnight

Judas escaped into the darkness, choosing his path as carefully as he could in the moonlight. He flinched at every breeze, sure the others had noticed his absence and discerned his intent. They would try to stop him. None of them would believe Jesus had lost faith.

The signs were there, if anyone was paying attention. That no one *was* paying attention was exactly why Judas fled toward Jerusalem under cover of darkness. They would say *he* had lost faith. But Judas, son of Simon, had not lost faith. He knew beyond question that Jesus was the promised Messiah. This was the rock on which he had built his hopes. He would not lose faith—even if Jesus himself had.

Sunday

The week had been tumultuous, to say the least, overstuffed with harbingers of the approaching Day, if—like Judas—one were inclined to read signs and portents into events. *Not that one has to be a magician,* Judas reflected. *Subtlety has never been Jesus' strength, and he has abandoned all pretense on the road to Jerusalem.*

On the day he knew Pilate would march into Jerusalem from the west, Jesus entered from the east. The Roman parade was all cavalry and soldiers, banners and imperial standards, a show of power to remind the pilgrims celebrating the Passover that Caesar was no pharaoh tossed so easily into the sea. Jesus' parade was all Galilean peasants waving palm branches and singing triumphal hymns. Pilate entered on a white stallion; Jesus rode a donkey. If Rome took note at all, it saw no threat. But the Galileans and Judeans all knew the words of Zechariah: "Lo, your king comes to you; triumphant and victorious is he, humble and riding on a donkey." In one fell swoop, Jesus galvanized his Galilean supporters, declared his messiahship to Jerusalem, and mocked Rome. Judas had always marveled at Jesus' brilliance, but that parade was a masterstroke.

Following along behind Jesus, clapping and singing with the crowds, Judas marched into history. Only a few days earlier, the Twelve had argued who would be granted to sit at Jesus' right and left. The Sons of Thunder had actually *requested* it. But as they followed their king into the Holy City, the argument seemed trite to Judas. They all marched behind their messiah. *A thousand years from now,* he thought, *our descendants will tell stories of their great-great-great-grandfathers who marched into Jerusalem and into glory, who defeated Rome and established the kingdom of heaven on earth. And who would be named among us? Me!*

Perhaps delirium has blinded the other disciples to the signs, Judas thought. He noted how quiet Jesus was in the midst of the celebration. When they visited the temple that day, Jesus had looked around the Court of the Gentiles, carefully taking inventory of the layout. His silence on the road back to Bethany that night had been uncharacteristic. The others laughed and joked, unable to see through the haze of anticipated glory. But Judas saw.

Monday

The fig tree caught them all off guard. Jesus seemed inexplicably irritated that he hadn't found any figs. After he cursed the tree, Andrew approached him. "Lord, what's wrong? You know it's not the season for figs."

Jesus sighed heavily. "Yes, Andrew. But some things should always be in season." The Twelve were used to cryptic responses from him, so they nodded and exchanged the usual hapless looks. They assumed—rightly, as it turned out—that Jesus would explain it to them later.

As they crested the Mount of Olives, they paused, as they did each time, to marvel at the temple. Judas's heart quickened at the sight of the temple sitting atop Mount Zion, glowing in the sunlight. From that vantage point, it was obvious the beautiful, enormous structure was the very footstool of the Lord.

They descended to Jerusalem through the East Gate at the foot of the Temple Mount then entered the Court of the Gentiles, already packed with pilgrims preparing for the Passover. Jerusalem, a huge city on any day, was never so full as at Passover, and the temple was the hub of the Passover activity. Thousands pressed within the walls, changing Roman denarii for Jewish coins, buying and selling animals.

One moment, Judas was lost in the sights, sounds, and smells of the crowd. The next, he heard shouting, and after scanning the throngs of people, found Jesus turning over tables and quoting prophets. He shook open cages to release doves, untied and whipped lambs, swept piles of carefully stacked coins from tables into the crowds of pilgrims. The merchants were shouting as well, some attempting to argue with him, others calling for the temple guard.

Several priests pushed through the crowd, and no sooner had they broken through to confront Jesus than he stopped and turned to them. He shouted, "It is written, 'My house shall be called a house of prayer,' but you are making it a den of robbers."

Jesus refused to allow the merchants to gather their animals, though several tried to pry their coins from the hands of pilgrims who had scooped them up. The priests whispered among themselves and finally sent for instructions from their superiors. Word spread quickly throughout the temple complex that the rabbi from the Galilee was there.

Before anyone could figure out what to do with Jesus, the Court of the Gentiles was flooded with the blind and lame. As he always did, Jesus began healing. Men who had been unable to enter the temple for years were brought to him and healed. They immediately ran to the priests to be declared clean. An air of celebration began to spread throughout the courtyard as more and more people found healing. Someone—probably Philip or Bartholomew—began singing the same messianic psalms they had sung as they entered the city.

It was hard not to get swept up in the euphoria. The Messiah had ridden into Jerusalem, and there he was, in the Lord's own house, acting out the Jubilee year. Judas felt swept along in the riptide of history in the making. No one seemed to note the fear in the eyes of the merchants and the priests. No one saw the leaders of the Pharisees and the Herodians whispering together at the edges of the courtyard. No one except Judas—and Jesus, of course, who saw everything.

Tuesday

The next morning, on their way into the city, they noticed the fig tree withered and dead, its leaves a crown of death spread on the ground. The Twelve began whispering to one another as they noticed it, but it was Peter who spoke up. "Rabbi, look! The fig tree that you cursed has withered."

Jesus slowed and turned to them. Only once before—when Jesus had learned that his cousin John had been executed—had Judas seen such weariness in his rabbi's face. He looked as though he were Samson carrying the gates of Gaza up Hebron, but without Samson's great strength.

"You must have faith in God." He looked down toward the temple sitting atop Mount Zion. "Believe me, if you say to this mountain, 'Be raised up and thrown into the sea,' and you do not doubt for one moment, but believe that what you say will happen, it will be done for you." He turned back to the Twelve. "Prayer, children. Prayer. Whatever you ask in prayer, believe and it will be yours."

As they descended toward Jerusalem, Judas reflected on his rabbi's opaque, troubling words. *Why would anyone want to cast Zion into the sea? Babylon destroyed Solomon's Temple but cannot destroy Mount Zion. Even Rome cannot destroy Zion.* A scrap of song leaped into Judas's mind, and it seemed particularly appropriate in that historic week.

Judas elbowed Peter, walking next to him, and muttered just loud enough for Peter to hear, "God is our refuge and strength."

Peter smiled, and a song erupted from his lips, characteristically booming and off-key:

A very present help in trouble.
Therefore we will not fear, though the earth should change,

> though the mountains shake in the heart of the sea;
> though its waters roar and foam,
> though the mountains tremble with its tumult.

Peter's mirth spread, and soon the rest of the Twelve joined in. But Judas quickly trailed off. *Does no one else notice that Jesus is not singing with us?*

They returned to the temple, and Judas was not surprised to see they were awaited; several prominent Pharisees huddled at the edge of the courtyard. When they saw Jesus, they began speaking hurriedly together. Judas saw them conspiring with another group of men he recognized as Herodians. Only days before, seeing those two groups conspiring would have filled Judas with righteous pity. The enemy of their enemy makes them friends, but what hope have the enemies of the Messiah? Today, however, Judas couldn't ignore the subtle shadow of dread cast by Jesus' increasingly strange behavior.

Judas was so focused on the conspirators he didn't see the envoy emerge from the temple. But as the murmuring around him swelled, he turned to see the crowd parting and a large group of priests and scribes coming directly toward Jesus and the Twelve. It seemed as though everyone but the high priest Caiaphas himself was marching toward them. Jesus' eyes were hard, and the weariness from earlier was gone or at least hidden from view.

One of the chief priests stepped forward. "Hear now, you troublemaker. You may not just march in here and disrupt the Passover proceedings."

Jesus smiled thinly. "I see you received my message." He looked around the courtyard. "I also see you have yet to drive the thieves out from my father's house."

"Yes, yes. You're a prophet. We're all *deeply* impressed, I assure you." The priest's sarcasm was thick, and several of his company chuckled their agreement. "Tell me, *prophet,* by whose authority are you doing these things? Who gave you the authority to walk in here and start tossing tables?"

Judas recognized the trap. If Jesus claimed divine authority there before the leaders of the temple, they could have him arrested. Judas cursed himself as a fool. *We should have been prepared for this. This might be* the *moment Jesus declares himself! And we did not bring swords; we did not coordinate with the men who came down from Galilee with us.*

Before Judas could do more than panic, Jesus said to the chief priest, "Answer a question for me, and I will answer yours. Was John's baptism of heaven, or was it only a human invention?"

The chief priest frowned, and after thinking for a moment, he turned to consult his friends. Judas noted suddenly that many in the Court of the Gentiles were watching this showdown, and he had no doubt many of them had received John's baptism. Judas marveled again at Jesus' quick reply. If they denied John was a true prophet, they would lose credibility with the crowd. But if they admitted John was of heaven, Jesus could ask why they had refused his call to repentance. Either way, they weakened their position as leaders of the temple.

Finally the priest turned again to Jesus, "We don't know."

Jesus smiled. "You couldn't discern the truth of John's ministry? No wonder you struggle with mine."

Judas watched their faces turn red. Several pulled on their beards and whispered angrily to one another. But none dared challenge him publicly again. Jesus began to teach the crowds, telling his signature parables, but this time painting the religious leaders in Jerusalem as dangerous, corrupt, and ungodly. It wasn't long before half the courtyard was listening to him—including many of the scribes and priests, as well as some Sadducees, Pharisees, and Herodians. Again and again, they asked him questions, posing as friendly, but each question was a carefully laid trap that sought to discredit him. Again and again, Jesus danced among their traps and left them ensnared instead.

By the midday meal, no one dared ask him any questions, and when the crowd began to drift away, Jesus dismissed them all. He led the Twelve out of the temple, through the Sheep Gate. Judas lost himself in the columns, towers, and stone. "Look, Rabbi! These stones are so large! Have you ever worked with anything so impressive? Surely the craftsmanship is unequaled. No wonder this temple is the envy of the world. Truly a fitting house for the Lord!"

Jesus turned back and scanned the temple gate, taking in the whole complex with his carpenter's gaze. His shoulders sagged, and he said, "Do you see these great buildings? Not one of these magnificent stones will be left standing upon its brother. Every single rock and beam will be utterly destroyed."

Then he turned and continued out of the city. None of them spoke. What could they say? Judas's mind raced. *This temple has stood as long as Solomon's and after Herod's renovations was grander by far—more than five hundred years since Babylon destroyed the Holy City. True, Rome is more powerful than Babylon ever had been, but isn't that why the Messiah has come now? To conquer God's enemies? To preserve God's people? To defend God's house?*

Doubt grew like a weed in Judas's mind as he recalled Jesus' words by the fig tree. "If you say to this mountain, 'Be raised up and thrown into the sea,' it will be done for you."

Once they were free of the city, Andrew asked Jesus what he had meant by his prophecy. But Jesus' reply clarified nothing. He promised not conquest and victory but persecution, arrest, and betrayal. He foretold a desolating sacrilege, the enemies of God standing in the holy of holies as Pompeii had a century before. He promised suffering on a scale not known since Noah and the unmaking of creation. As they were passing the fig tree yet again, he gestured to it. "You know when this tree blooms, summer is here. So too, keep watch for these signs. The end of the world is at hand. Some among you will live to see it."

They said nothing else on the way back to Bethany, but Jesus' final words echoed over and over in Judas's mind. *Keep watch.* Judas was watching, and what he saw was a man being crushed by the weight of his own mission. Jesus was cracking. He was supposed to challenge Rome—as he had when he rode into the city. But he had spent the past two days enraging the Jewish leaders, turning many in the city against him. And he was calling for the destruction of the temple, for the unmaking of creation.

As he followed his rabbi, his messiah, Judas thought of wind and waves obeying Jesus' command. Of unclean spirits fleeing at a word. Of countless eyes opened and tongues loosened. Of the dead raised.

But in the slump of Jesus' shoulders, Judas saw no power. He saw doubt—or worse: defeat.

Tuesday Night

That night, a man named Simon hosted a feast in their honor. Jesus had cured him of leprosy at the temple the previous day, and Simon spared no expense for the meal. He proved to be an excellent host. The cushions on which they reclined were comfortable; the slaves were attentive and unobtrusive as they washed feet and served the food, which was well prepared. Judas gathered that before his illness, Simon had been a man of some prominence in Jerusalem, perhaps a Pharisee. But even though a temple priest had declared him clean after the healing, Judas saw none of Jerusalem's religious elite present for the feast. *Not surprising after the confrontation today.* A heavy foreboding lay just beneath all the talk and laughter around the table.

Suddenly the smell of death filled Judas's nostrils. He nearly gagged as the air became thick with nard. Unbidden, images flooded his mind: Preparing his mother's body for burial. The wailing of the mourners as they laid his grandfather in the family tomb. The baby brother who died before he could walk.

Judas looked back to see a woman he didn't recognize cradling a jar of nard in her hands and pouring it carefully over Jesus' feet. At first he thought she must be a slave, but she was not dressed as a slave. He noted the size and craftsmanship of the jar. *That nard must be worth at least a year's wages.*

Those at the table began to simmer with confusion and disgust. Suddenly the whole area smelled like a funeral procession, the potent nard overwhelming the fragrance of the lamb and sauces. Judas could see he was not the only person who had lost his appetite, but none of them was sure what to do. Even Simon looked to Jesus, seated at his right in the place of honor.

But Jesus' eyes were closed in silent meditation. He sat back from the table and allowed the woman to pour the nard over his head as well. As she rubbed the oil into his hair, Jesus opened his eyes, and they were damp. The tension Judas had seen in his rabbi's shoulders seemed to fall away, and for a moment Jesus looked like nothing more than a baby cradled in his mother's lap. He looked peaceful for the first time since they had arrived in Judea.

Judas felt fury rising in his chest. With tensions as high as they were, her display was in poor taste, even for a rabbi who routinely flouted gender propriety. He leaped to his feet. "Rabbi, what is the meaning of this?" The voices of some of the other Twelve joined his protest.

Jesus closed his eyes again and spoke, his voice weary. "Leave her alone, Judas. She has performed a great kindness for me."

Peter objected, "But, Lord! Such a waste! We could've sold that nard for at least three hundred denarii!"

Someone else chimed in. "Think of all the poor we could help with so much money!"

Jesus seemed not to have heard them for several long moments. Finally he sighed, "You will always have the poor with you. You can show them kindness whenever you wish. But you will not always have me."

Judas was stunned. *You will not always have me?*

Jesus continued. "She has prepared my body for burial. In the years to come, wherever the good news is proclaimed—anywhere in the world—what she has just done will be celebrated as an act of great faithfulness."

He turned to the woman and thanked her, then reclined once more at the table to resume eating. After casting furtive glances at each other, Simon and the Twelve began to pick at their food. Slowly conversation returned, though more strained than ever.

Judas, however, said nothing. He found he could not eat with the cloying smell of death emanating so strongly from Jesus.

Tuesday Midnight

The way down the Mount of Olives had been harrowing in the moonlight, but Judas now stood before the East Gate. An extra coin to the guard ensured his message reached the high priest's house, and he didn't have to wait long to be admitted into the city. As Judas entered the city, he reflected on the toll he had seen

Jerusalem take on Jesus. The crowds. The priests. The merchants in the temple. *But of course the city is mired in sin! Why else must the Messiah come?*

Jesus' words at the meal echoed in Judas ear. "She has prepared my body for burial."

Judas arrived outside Caiaphas's house and called out. A bleary-eyed slave answered, and Judas said, "I am Judas, son of Simon, called Iscariot by Jesus of Nazareth. Tell your master I bring the solution to his problem." The slave grumbled but retreated into the house. Soon Judas heard the sounds of the household coming to life.

He nearly fled back into the darkness, but the smell of the nard seemed to cling to him. The weariness in Jesus' eyes haunted him. Jesus' words, "You will not always have me," had chased him to the city, and now they held him there. Judas thought Jesus had lost faith in himself. *But I have not, cannot, lose faith in Jesus.*

Before the dinner with Jesus had ended, Judas had made his decision. If Jesus would not act, Judas would force his hand. If Jesus would not enact heaven's kingdom on earth, Judas would.

Finally Judas was shown into a private chamber where Caiaphas sat with several other men whom Judas recognized from the temple courtyard earlier in the day. He had clearly interrupted important business. Without waiting to be announced, Judas spoke. "I have come to deliver Jesus of Nazareth, who some call the Messiah, into your hands."

Several of the men whispered to one another in shock, but Caiaphas's eyes narrowed, appraising this stranger. "And why should we believe you, son of Simon? You are a known follower of the Nazarene." Caiaphas's tone revealed his contempt for Jesus' humble origins.

"Listen to the shape of my words, noble Caiaphas," Judas said. "I grew up near Hebron. My people have known the rule of the

Herodians and the power of Rome. It is true that in recent years I have been following Jesus. You have seen with your own eyes his power to work miracles. You have witnessed firsthand the power in his words." Judas saw one of the scribes frown at this barb and knew he must tread carefully. "But as the Passover drew near, we noticed a change in Jesus. I believe he aspires to be the Messiah some think him to be."

Judas concealed his lie as a tare among grains of truth. "I am the only man from among the Twelve who has lived outside Galilee. These are simple men with simple ideas about the kingdom of heaven. They do not understand as we do in the South the power of Rome, of the delicate balance we must strike to remain faithful to God in the shadow of Caesar. A messianic revolt can only end in disaster for our people. Jesus must be stopped."

Caiaphas snorted. "Your words are honey, Iscariot. How do we know this is not a trap? Perhaps you wish to embarrass us, to give credibility to your messiah." His final word dripped with disdain.

Judas shrugged. "So don't let him choose the confrontation. My master does not share his plans with us, but I fear for the day of Passover. What better day for the Messiah to reveal himself?"

And then Judas sprang his trap. "You must stop him. Tomorrow night. We will eat the Passover meal in the city. I can deliver him to you afterward, when we are returning to Bethany. Send the Temple Guard. You can take him outside the city, at night, away from the crowds. You have seen his followers. We are no army; most of us have held only the dull, rusted swords of our fathers. We are no match for the Temple Guard."

Then Judas smiled. "Unless Jesus truly is the Messiah, in which case it hardly matters whether you take him tomorrow night or wait for him to announce himself."

Several of the priests spat or pulled at their beards, but Caiaphas said nothing. He held up his hand to silence his fellows. "Why would you betray your master, Iscariot?"

"I have seen Jesus do much good. He gives hope to the poor. He heals the sick. He frees those oppressed by unclean spirits. And he calls us all to love God more. I would not see this end." Then Judas lied easily, because it was no lie at all. "I love my master with all my heart. I wish to save him from himself."

Caiaphas grunted. "Such devotion is admirable. Leave us, son of Simon. You will have your answer shortly."

Judas followed the slave back to the courtyard of Caiaphas's house, his heart pounding in his chest. Caiaphas was true to his word. One of the scribes came to Judas, gripped his arm, and whispered into his ear, "Come to us tomorrow night. You will be richly rewarded for your efforts." Then he retreated inside as quickly as he had come.

Judas barely remembered returning to Bethany, and long after he sneaked back to his pallet, he lay awake, head filled with visions of glory. *Tomorrow night, the enemies of the Messiah will strike. By Friday, the whole of Jerusalem will see Jesus exalted as God's anointed. And who will be at his right side? Who else but the man who did not lose faith, even when Jesus himself did? Who else but the man who had the courage to follow Jesus' mission all the way to the end?*

When Judas finally fell asleep, only the words of the scribe rang in his ears. "You will be richly rewarded for your efforts."

12

WHAT DEATH SMELLS LIKE

The Betrayal of Faithfulness

As a pastor, I visit a lot of hospitals and nursing homes, and they all smell the same. Pungent, medicinal eucalyptus covers the faint but unmistakable odors of our mortality: urine, feces, blood, and death. Walking down the hall at a hospital reveals how powerful our sense of smell is. As the fragrances of our human weakness waft into our nostrils, memories flood our minds.

Maybe you sat with a family member as she struggled through a chronic illness or with a friend who just found out he had only months to live. You watched as chemotherapy ravaged the body of your child. Or you had to turn off a machine that was keeping your parent alive. Plenty of people simply won't go to hospitals because the memories those smells conjure up for them are too painful. (There's a reason Yankee doesn't sell a hospital-scented candle.) Ultimately that smell is the smell of mortality, of the breaking down of our bodies, of death.

Death is the one great equalizer. No matter how much money we have, no matter how powerful our military, no matter how safe we play it, we all die in the end. That knowledge makes most of us afraid, so our culture has done everything it can to shield us from pain, the harbinger of our mortality.

We quarantine our elderly and infirm in hospitals and homes so they can die out of sight and therefore out of mind.

We buy our meat in sealed packages that look nothing like the animals they came from. We consume them happily, blissfully ignorant of the deplorable and inhumane conditions in which the animals were raised.

When tragedy strikes, we click the sad emoticon on Facebook or retweet a news story on Twitter. We set up a temporary profile picture assuring the world we are "PRAYING FOR ______." If someone has set up a number to text, we might give ten dollars to the earthquake/tsunami/hurricane/shooting victims' fund. Then we forget and go about our business.

We design systems to shield us from pain, from the reality of death. Religion is one of those systems. Church attendance here in the United States spiked after 9/11 because people were afraid. We felt vulnerable and powerless, so we went to listen to someone tell us God loves us and is in control. In that way, we were not unlike Judas and his contemporaries, clinging to the promise of a messiah because it gave them hope to endure under Roman oppression. Our own discomfort with death helps us empathize with Judas.

Worst. Human. Ever.

The Bible tells us little about Judas. We get no story for his call. John tells us he is the "son of Simon Iscariot" (John 6:71). The meaning of "Iscariot" has long been debated. The most popular theory, also corroborated by some ancient copies of John's Gospel, is that it means "man of Kerioth."[1] In this case, much like Mary Magdalene, whose title means "from Magdala," and Jesus of Nazareth, Judas was identified by his hometown or possibly the hometown of his father.[2]

However Judas ended up living in the Galilee, his call was probably similar to those of the rest of the Twelve. He began to follow a provocative new rabbi who worked miracles, irritated those in power, and taught authoritatively about the imminent arrival of God's kingdom. Soon this rabbi handpicked him to be part of the inner circle of twelve, and it became increasingly obvious Jesus viewed himself as some sort of harbinger of this new kingdom. Eventually the Twelve figured out that Jesus believed himself to be the actual Messiah, and to their own surprise, they believed it too.

The so-called confession at Caesarea Philippi is a turning point in Mark's Gospel (Mark 8:27–9:1). Jesus asked the Twelve who people were saying he was and then asked them directly what they thought. Peter blurted out what was on all their minds: Jesus is the Messiah. What has been obvious to those of us reading Mark's Gospel—with its opening line announcing "the good news of Jesus Christ, the Son of God"—is only now, halfway through the story, spoken aloud by the Twelve. Peter's confession was a stake in the ground. Jesus confirmed that he was Israel's long-awaited Messiah, and for his followers, there was no going back.

Messianic expectations in Jesus' day were diverse, but everyone looking for a messiah was looking for some variation of the same theme: a ruler who would be even greater than David, Israel's greatest king.[3] For more than five hundred years, God's people had lived in exile. Even after they were allowed to return from captivity to rebuild the temple and Jerusalem's walls, they were a vassal state. And though they achieved independence under the Hasmonean king-priests, that dynasty was divisive, tumultuous, and bitterly brief.

By Jesus' day, Israel was squarely under the boot of Rome. Israel's kings had always been warrior-kings, so the Jewish people were constantly on the lookout for a mighty warrior to lead the armies of God against all of Israel's enemies. The Messiah would take back David's throne and rule in peace and justice. By Jesus' day, plenty of would-be messiahs had raised armies, opposed Rome, and found themselves hanging on crosses outside the city.

But Jesus was different. He worked miracles—not just healings and exorcism but also miracles that affected nature itself. He demonstrated total dominion over even the forces of evil. And his teachings were unlike anything anyone had heard before. Again and again, he challenged the powerful and gathered the poor and oppressed. He danced past every trap and outsmarted every opponent. And eventually his followers figured out he was Israel's promised Messiah.

The problem was that their picture of the Messiah was wrong. Jesus did not come to conquer as a mighty warrior. He came to die, to give his life for the good of the whole world. Mark used a bizarre story to warn us not to get excited that the Twelve had finally figured out that Jesus was the Messiah.

Immediately before Peter's confession, Mark tells us a story neither Matthew nor Luke include in their Gospels (Mark 8:22-26).[4] Jesus came across a blind man who begged to be healed. Jesus healed him, and the man reported he could see—but only sort of. "I can see people, but they look like trees" (v. 24). So Jesus healed him again, and then the man could see perfectly. What was going on there? Did Jesus not zap him hard enough the first time? Did he get distracted? Maybe the man was blind but *also* had an astigmatism, so Jesus had to cure him of two separate ailments.

No, Mark was warning us. When Peter confessed, "You are the Messiah" he was right, but neither he nor the rest of the Twelve saw Jesus clearly (Mark 8:29). They had an out-of-focus picture of what the Messiah had come to do. We know that because, after Peter's confession, Jesus told them the game plan: he was going to Jerusalem to die and be raised from the dead.

Then Peter pulled Jesus aside to set him straight. You can imagine the lecture. "Jesus, enough of this 'I'm going to die!' talk. Yes, things are tense, but you're the Messiah! God promised you victory! You're our king, our mighty warrior. We're going to go to Jerusalem, and you're going to crush the enemies of God! We're all behind you."

Jesus rebuked Peter with the famous phrase, "Get behind me, Satan!" (v. 33).[5]

For Mark, it was impossible to understand the kind of Messiah Jesus was until he saw him crucified. This is why, throughout Mark's Gospel, Jesus warned people not to tell anyone he was the Messiah.[6] And it's why the moment after Jesus died, a Roman soldier at the foot of his cross exclaimed, "Truly this man was God's Son!" (Mark 15:39).

The Twelve could see Jesus' messianic identity, but not clearly. They needed more than just that confession to see the kind of messiah Jesus is. They needed a second touch, and they'd get it at the cross.

But Judas wouldn't be there because of how Jesus smelled.

The Odor of Betrayal

The key moment for Judas gets almost no attention in the church. You won't find it on most timelines of Holy Week, and it sometimes doesn't even get its own italicized header in study Bibles (that's how you *really* know it doesn't matter). But immediately after Jesus was anointed at the house of Simon the Leper, Judas went to the chief priests to betray him. Why would this anointing be Judas's turning point?

The tensions the Twelve experienced during Holy Week are nearly unimaginable. Jesus staged the triumphal entry to make a mockery of Pilate and his Roman legions. To any Jewish people watching, the signals were clear: Jesus was declaring himself to be the Messiah, here to challenge Rome's power and authority.

But instead of confronting Rome, Jesus turned on his own people. He cleansed the temple and challenged the chief priests and scribes, publicly humiliating them. Even privately, the Twelve must have thought Jesus was acting strange. He cursed a fig tree for not bearing fruit, even though figs weren't in season. And when the Galilean peasants marveled at the glory of Herod's temple, the envy of nations and gods all over the world, Jesus announced it would be destroyed—not one stone left on another (Mark 13:2). His description of the Day of the Lord—the day of the Messiah's coming conquest, foretold for centuries by prophets—was not a vision of victory but of devastation.

For the Jewish people, the temple was the bridge between heaven and earth, the religious and ideological center of the universe. If God's throne is in the heavenly throne room, the temple was God's footstool, where the physical presence of God lived among God's people.[7] The temple was the Jewish people's source of life, hope, and security. They could not have imagined a messiah ruling without a temple. So Jesus' prediction of the temple's destruction—just days after he led a victory march into Jerusalem and in the midst of dangerous tensions with the religious elite—did not sound like a brave new world. It sounded like Jesus was giving up, like he thought his messianic mission was doomed to fail.

And then Simon hosted a banquet for Jesus. We know little about Simon and less about the mysterious woman who anointed Jesus. According to Mark and Matthew, Simon was a leper. Presumably Jesus had recently healed him—a great reason to throw a party in his honor. The woman simply appeared at the fringes of the party. We never even learn her name.[8]

The woman broke a jar of nard over Jesus. The Twelve claimed to be angry at the cost of the nard, which was somewhere in the neighborhood of a year's wages. But the nard she used was a burial ointment, as strong perfumes were used in funeral rites to cover the smell of decomposition.

This means that, for the next several days, Jesus walked around smelling like a funeral parlor. No wonder the Twelve were upset. The woman essentially poured gasoline on a smoldering fire. Worse, rather than rebuke her, Jesus praised her faithfulness, again embracing the possibility that he was going to die soon. For Judas, this proved to be too much. Mark tells us that immediately after *this* event, Judas decided to betray Jesus.

True Believer

We can't imagine how one of Jesus' inner circle could betray him, so we project onto Judas. We assume he must have been a snake from the beginning; he was nothing but evil from head to toe. By ignoring the story Mark is telling, we miss what drove Judas to do the unthinkable.[9]

What if we assume Judas saw himself as a faithful follower of Jesus? Can we imagine that he was wholly committed to Jesus' messianic mission? What if Judas's sin wasn't that he was a mole or a wolf among sheep, but rather a religious idolater? As Mark hinted, Judas may have been faithful, but to the *wrong* messiah.

The Twelve gave up everything to follow Jesus. They left their families and their livelihoods, and they abandoned their place in the world because Jesus promised them a new world, a better world. They believed him, they followed him, and they came to realize he was the long-awaited Messiah.

For the Twelve, *messiah* meant conquest and glory, not shame and defeat. But during Holy Week, Judas watched Jesus crumbling. We who live on the other side of Golgotha recognize that, even then, he bore the weight of his impending crucifixion. But to Judas, it looked like Jesus was giving up, losing faith in God's promises. The scene at Simon's table sealed Judas's suspicions: Jesus allowed himself to be anointed for death and went around for the next few days smelling like it. It's like that scene in Westerns where the town undertaker starts measuring the hero for a coffin the day before the big gunfight at high noon, except this hero was helping pick out his coffin. Jesus had embraced his death. Judas could not.

If Judas believed Jesus was God's promised Messiah, and if Judas believed Jesus was losing faith in himself, he had only one option. Judas grabbed the wheel of history for himself. He betrayed his master and his messiah to the powers, confident that God would not fail, that at Jesus' arrest the very skies would open and the armies of heaven would swoop in to destroy the enemies of the Messiah.

Except that's not what happened. Jesus was not that kind of messiah then or now. Judas's picture of him had no room for suffering—only triumph. Judas could not conceive of a messiah who lost; his messiah could only be a victor. Judas committed himself to the wrong cause, and his legacy is eternal infamy.

I'm a Loser, Baby. So Why Don't You Kill Me?

Judas's story should give us all pause, especially when our picture of God is as triumphalist as his was. This God-who-wins isn't called Baal or Marduk or Ganesh. We call this God "Jesus." We claim he is the god to whom the Scriptures bear witness. This is despite Jesus' declaration in John's Gospel that God is most fully glorified when the Son is lifted up on the cross.[10]

Christians love to look toward the second coming to affirm our triumphalist narrative of God. As one popular megachurch pastor reflected on Jesus' appearance at the battle of Armageddon in Revelation 19, he gushed, "Jesus is a pride fighter with a tattoo down His leg, a sword in His hand and the commitment to make someone bleed. That is a guy I can worship. . . . I cannot worship a guy I can beat up."[11]

In this line of thinking, the cross is an embarrassment, an unfortunate hiccup in God's otherwise hypermasculine character. A god who dies must only allow this, because *in the end*, he'll get what's his.[12] Many cannot imagine worshiping a god who loses. This has been the case since the beginning. It's why Paul had to declare to the church in Rome, "I am not ashamed of the gospel" (Romans 1:16). But we are removed from Paul, and Christianity has become the dominant lens through which Western culture views the world. Crosses have become decorations and jewelry and tattoos.[13] We don't find it strange to take pride in the cross—but that's because the cross is no longer a tool of execution used by a hostile empire.[14]

But occasionally the smell of death makes its way into our carefully air-conditioned churches. On July 4, 2016, prominent Christian rapper Lecrae tweeted a picture of a group of black slaves standing in a cotton field. The caption read, "My family on July 4th 1776."[15] Immediately a fan responded, "Done supporting you bro. You make everything a race issue lately instead of a gospel issue. You promote guilt instead of love."[16] His response was only the first of many similar reactions from white Christians who were angry that he had dared suggest a connection between race and Jesus' good news.

White Christians often react with hostility to the introduction of race into religious conversations. We feel threatened because our position has been one of cultural privilege and power, and we view racial justice as a loss for white culture. And our triumphalist faith has not taught us to be prepared for loss. Our whitewashed Savior invites us to let him die *for* us so we can skip the cross and go straight to the resurrection.

The Jesus who commands us to love our neighbors as ourselves must care about race and racial inequality as well as how those inequalities—inherited from institutionalized slavery and Jim Crow—shape other institutions like criminal justice, education, access to healthy food, and even churches. We teach our kids to sing, "Red and yellow, black and white, all are precious in his sight." So we cannot, when confronted with the reality that all are not precious in the eyes of our culture, declare that race is not something God cares about.

Race is a difficult, delicate, divisive issue. But we cannot ignore that Sunday morning continues to be the most segregated hour of our week. White Christians like me cannot turn our backs on our brothers and sisters of color for the sake of a privatized, individualistic religion. We triumphalists want to pretend that our churches fell out of the sky twenty years ago.

It's painful to acknowledge that our culture is built on a bedrock of imperialism, slavery, and genocide. The bodies of the oppressed lie rotting, and whenever the scent of death begins to waft up into our lives, we turn to religion to make it go away. Whenever a person of color insists that her life matters in a culture that acts otherwise, we gather in our segregated worship spaces to remind ourselves God loves us, and as long as we talk about Jesus, we don't have to talk about anything going on in the world.

Race is only one area where our churches are uncomfortable with loss. We could talk about gender inequality. Or the consumerist church-shopping our competing activities encourage. Or our discomfort with basic spiritual practices like charity and service. We made church easy so as not to offend, lest our flock seek out greener pastures and find out the shepherd across the way has a better light show and funnier jokes.

Have we strayed far from Judas? Like Judas, we have no room in our picture of God for death, for loss, for weakness. We commit to our picture of God not because that picture is true but because our God tells us we're good and moral. This God doesn't require us to change, to consider the possibility we are wrong. This God doesn't ask us to pick up our crosses and follow him anywhere. He calls us winners and assures us that he will battle on our behalf and vanquish every foe.

Practice Makes Perfect

What are we to do? How can we be certain we have not created a false god? Mark gave us the antidote: As with the Twelve, we must follow Jesus to the cross. Rather than flee from the smell of death, we must embrace it. Death takes many forms, but among the most painful is the death of our certainty.[17]

The triumphalist god loves certainty—the conviction that we are purely, wholly, unassailably right. When someone challenges us, we rush to defend our position, to consolidate followers, to cover over the discomfort, and to remind ourselves that we're right and God is still on our side.

We've become skilled at shielding ourselves from the possibility of weakness, from the scent of death wafting into our lives. But if we are to follow Jesus to the cross—rather than run for the hills as the Twelve did, or try to do God's work for him, as Judas did—we must embrace the pain of death. We must be prepared to receive it as the path to life.

Imagine if Judas had been less certain he was right about Jesus. Imagine if his faith had some room for doubt. Imagine if he had been standing with Peter on that beach when Jesus asked Peter three times whether he loved him, inviting three confessions to match Peter's three denials (John 21:15-19). How would Jesus have reconciled with Judas? A kiss? An embrace? If only Judas had experienced the forgiveness and love the other Twelve had. Then he would not be the greatest of villains. He would be the patron saint of all those who were too committed to the wrong image of God until Jesus' death freed them.

The early churches had to deal with many of the same issues we do. They were racially mixed. They operated in a culture that didn't share their values. And we can see in the New Testament how they engaged these issues (see, for example, Acts 15:1-35; Romans 14:7-13; 1 Corinthians 12–13). They prayed together. They listened to one another. They committed to unity above all else and respected those with whom they had differences as valued members of the same body.

I struggle with triumphalism and certainty; no one has ever accused me of wallowing in self-doubt. I like to say (usually with a smirk), "I think I'm right about everything, but I know I'm not." I committed a long time ago to listen more than I speak and to work hard to understand someone who disagrees with me. This means I spend a lot of time asking questions and keeping my opinions to myself. Each time I choose to keep my mouth shut, I'm dying a little death to my own certainty, to my idolatrous triumphalism.

Any time I find myself scratching my head and wondering, "How could they think *that*?" I turn to social media. I find four or five thoughtful people who hold *that* position, and I follow them. I commit to listen, especially when what they say makes me uncomfortable. I position myself as a student. I ask questions, and I don't lecture.

Often I still disagree with the people or the position. But I always find a deeper level of respect and—particularly among the people in my congregation—a more intimate sense of community. We love each other not *despite* our differences but *because of* them. Giving up my certainty hasn't hurt me. Surrendering to the death of my convictions has given me more pastoral authority, a stronger faith, and a better understanding of the God who would die for us and calls us to die as well.

Who will we be: Judas, who fled from the smell of death into the arms of Jesus' enemies, or the nameless, faithful woman, who saw Jesus clearly, who knew exactly what kind of God he was and who played her own small role in his mission?

As we die a thousand little deaths, we follow Jesus toward the cross. Our life becomes, in Paul's words, the fragrance of death to the world around us:

> Thanks be to God, who in Christ always leads us in triumphal procession, and through us spreads in every place the fragrance that comes from knowing him. For we are the aroma of Christ to God among those who are being saved and among those who are perishing; to the one a fragrance from death to death, to the other a fragrance from life to life. Who is sufficient for these things? (2 Corinthians 2:14-16)

God is the ultimate iconoclast, always bursting through false images of God we construct. Jesus is the God who is beyond all our boxes, the God who cannot be constrained by our false images.[18] Instead, when we surrender to this God, when we follow Jesus to the cross, we become a fragrance of life.

INTERLUDE

THE MONSTER AT THE END OF THIS BOOK

We're getting closer to the end of the book, and we have only one villain left: Satan, also called the devil. In some ways, Satan is unique. He is the only nonhuman villain, and he has unique access to God. Yet in important ways, Satan is the same as the other villains we have encountered. He was created good, then something happened to turn him against God.

Scholars have known for a long time that the most popular story of Satan's fall—that he is Lucifer, who rebelled before creation—is not a good accounting of what the Scriptures actually say about Satan. (More on that in just a few pages.)

Unfortunately the Bible isn't clear on exactly what happened—which we should expect to some degree, given that we're using human words and ideas to express activity in the heavenly realm. That said, what follows is my attempt to ask how Satan became the devil. Ultimately the answer to this question is unknowable. If God thought it was important, the Scriptures would be clearer on it.

As we've done with all the people in the stories so far, we're going to practice empathy—not for their sake, but for ours. If we can find some empathy even for the devil, maybe we can reach across the aisle and do the difficult work of empathizing with the other side. After all, they're not the devil—they're just humans!

So with no further ado, turn the page with me, and let's meet the monster at the end of the book, the devil who was once Satan, the Accuser.

13

SATAN

After the Temptation

The Accuser landed outside the throne room, his legions in tow. He furled his wings and hurried through the golden columns. He did not wish to compound his failure by arriving late to the Audience.

He heard, "Hail, Accuser!" and turned and saw the Healer rushing toward him across the grand portico. He sighed and strode through the gilded archway, and the Healer embraced him warmly. "You're late, Accuser! Because you spoke with him, yes? What is he like?"

A strong hand gripped the Accuser's shoulder, and the Strength's voice boomed out, "Yes, tell us, Accuser. Do not flaunt your status before us. We are envious enough as it is." As usual, the Strength seemed moments away from a hearty laugh.

"Status? I spend my days walking the earth. Have you been enjoying wine, Strength?" the Accuser asked.

Now the Strength did laugh, deep and joyful, though the Accuser's joke had not been particularly funny. "Wine indeed! The humans are not all bad. Are they, my friends?" He paused. "But come, Accuser. You alone have spoken with The Name since he became flesh. Truly you are The Name's favored son, though you are made and not begotten." The Strength laughed as heartily as before, this time at his own wit.

"I doubt very much my report will please The Name this day, Strength."

The Healer frowned. "You have come from testing him, yes? Did something happen? What is he like in person? Is he—much changed from before?"

The Accuser frowned. "No. He's not different. I mean, he is different—of course he's different but—" The Accuser struggled for words. "He is The Name."

"It is time."

Before the Accuser could continue, the Incomparable strode past him toward the throne room. The three exchanged a wry look but said nothing else. They fell in behind the Incomparable, followed by their legions in tight ranks, wings furled.

As they entered the throne room, a familiar awe eroded the Accuser's worry. No matter how often he entered into The Name's presence, no matter how many millennia since his first report, every moment he stood in the throne room he felt as though every atom of his being sang in perfect harmony with the whole of creation.

The Favored flew around the throne, chanting as always, their great animal forms shifting constantly—now a lion, now an eagle, now a human. Below them, the Burning chanted a countermelody, deep and powerful. But the light of their flame paled in comparison to the dancing pulses of light emanating from the throne in a rainbow of color. The throne itself flickered with lightning, and shockwaves of thunder rippled through the air, booming harmony to the chanting of The Name's angelic attendants. As the Accuser neared, he knelt, his gaze falling reverentially to the floor, a beautiful mosaic of gold and crystal.

The Name called out, beginning the old ritual. "Hail, Accuser! Where have you come from?"

The Accuser could hear the joy in The Name's greeting, and his worry ebbed further. He replied, as always, "From roaming about on the earth. From circling it whole."

"Rise, Accuser," The Name called. The Accuser complied and suddenly was at the foot of the throne, in the very seat of The Name. Welcome exuded palpably from The Name, a warm bath washing the dust of the earth from the Accuser's thoughts.

This was the moment for which the Accuser always longed—that feel of coming home, being washed clean, the stain of humanity rinsed away. No matter how far he traveled, no matter how foul the deeds to which he bore witness, to return and to kneel before The Name was to be renewed.

The Name whispered to him in tones reserved for secret conspirators, for brothers and mischief-makers, "You have done well, Accuser. You have outshone yourself today."

"I was defeated. I failed you." He knew his failure pleased The Name. *The faithful are his favorite—not because they do what he says, though that is good,* the Accuser thought. *The Name revels in humans who possess the strength of character to resist their baser desires. The Name loves the contest, the victory hard-won. Perhaps he loves them because they are so rare.*

"We could not discern his vice," he added. "The tests I prepared were not adequate. Next time I shall not fail."

The Name grinned, and his voice overflowed with delight. "Accuser, never has one of your tests been so carefully crafted, so perfectly tuned to human desire. That we did not fall is no failing of yours."

"I thought I had him. I was sure that atop that mountain, when he saw how easily he could have the world, he would fall. Power corrupts everyone, especially those born to be kings."

An old sadness diminished The Name's smile, if only for a moment. "You are nearly right, Accuser. Power corrupts most. It is a most delicious fruit. But we know the price of unearned power. Still, you did well, my faithful servant."

The Accuser frowned. "I took responsibility for his testing myself and did not discern his vice. Even Job did not pass every test. I will think on this and try again. Jesus is human. He cannot but fail."

"No." The Name voice was stern, woven through with joy and pride. "He is human. To be human is not to fail, but to soar. It is true, Adam's children have fallen. But he is the new Adam. His sons and daughters will be what they always should have been. You have proven him ready for what is to come. Now he must begin. Watch, Accuser. Watch and be amazed.

"Now, what of the rest?"

As always, the Accuser began his report of Israel's high priest. "Caiaphas is condemned for his pride, greed, and groveling. He licks the dust from Rome's boot, fills his storehouses, and then spits on his own people, all the while promising it's for their own good. Speaking of Rome, Pontius Pilate is condemned for his schemes and plots. Every person is a piece he moves about the board of his ambition. He loves only his wife."

At this, The Name smiled warmly. "Ah, Accuser, is his love for her not a thing of beauty? Would that it could be fanned into a fire that consumed his ambitions."

The Accuser frowned more deeply, but acquiesced. "Of course. A thing of beauty." He continued his report, every name a son of Adam or daughter of Eve. Every name a carefully accounted condemnation of their sins prepared by his legions. From time to time, The Name interrupted to comment on this person or that, each comment a wistful hope. No matter how vile, how wicked those humans were, The Name seemed only to see the good in them.

When the Accuser finished, The Name thanked him. "You do essential work, Accuser. Go with my love." And with that, his audience was over, and the Accuser found himself kneeling again, warm with the light of The Name's approval.

The Name proclaimed loudly to the assembled legions, "Behold, the Accuser, my faithful servant. I am well pleased with him."

The Name called, "Hail, Strength. Where have you come from?" But the Accuser barely heard it, his thoughts already turned to Jesus.

As the other archangels offered their reports and received their blessings, The Name's words echoed in the Accuser's mind: "He is the new Adam." *What game is The Name playing at now?*

After the Raising of Lazarus

The Accuser arrived to find the Healer and the Strength already talking excitedly together. When they saw the Accuser, they rushed to him. The Healer spoke first. "Four days Lazarus was in the grave, Accuser! Four days before The Name raised him! I have never seen such a thing. Even the widow's son was not dead three days before Elijah raised him."

The Strength growled his admiration as well. "Truly Jesus is awesome to behold. The unclean spirits flee before him, though he wields no sword. And he instructs the sea as he did in Egypt—indeed as when he first stretched the firmament and shaped the lands."

The Accuser frowned at them. "Yes. Jesus is—formidable. But he is not cautious. His enemies weary of having their hypocrisy exposed before their fellows. They have begun to conspire together. He forgets that flesh is more vulnerable than deity."

The Strength laughed. "What need has The Name for caution?" He swept his arm behind them. "Can he not summon all my legions at a word?"

The Incomparable strode in through the gates, his wings settling about his shoulders in a glowing cloak. He strode past, and the Healer rolled his eyes playfully. "Father has arrived; playtime is over, my brothers."

The archangels fell in behind the Incomparable and entered again into the throne room. The Accuser knelt and was summoned. "Hail, Accuser! Where have you come from?"

"From roaming about on the earth. From circling it whole."

"Rise, Accuser," The Name called. The Accuser complied, and in a moment he was in the midst of the throne. "Have you been watching, Accuser? Tell me what you see."

The Accuser related much the same report as he had given his compatriots. Everywhere Jesus went, life and flourishing followed. To trace his path was to trace cracks in the world through which The Name's kingdom leaked.

"But now he approaches Jerusalem. His enemies are numerous and powerful. Soon their hatred for him will overshadow their hatred for each other."

"Yes, all powers focus their gaze upon us. It is a heavy load to bear, Accuser."

"Can he—can you prevail? Your Twelve make for poor generals."

The Name laughed as deeply as the Strength ever did. "Accuser, always you tell the unpolished truth. Poor generals, you say?"

The Accuser frowned at The Name's mirth. "None of them is particularly intelligent. Nor are they charismatic—certainly not compared to Jesus himself. They are deeply flawed. Simon is condemned for his pride. His brother Andrew is condemned for his cowardice. Too often he will not speak up in the face of injustice—no surprise with a brother like Simon. The other two brothers are condemned for their wrath. Their tempers are as dry and fire-ready as kindling. Nathanael is condemned for faithlessness. He refuses to see good, even when it stares him in the face."

"Do you think so little of them all, Accuser?"

"How long did it take them to see he is the Messiah? And only then because Jesus asked them directly, 'Who do you say I am?' And now they squabble like hens over seed for who will be at his right and left. But they are not prepared for Jerusalem. They're village boys, not fit for the pits the city vipers haunt. Only Judas has any political savvy, and he is too pious by half to put it to any good use." The Accuser dropped his gaze. "My apologies. I know you love them."

The Name did not chastise him. "I do love them, Accuser. And you are not wrong about them. But perhaps you are blind to the good in them. They do not see yet, either. But they will soon. Soon everything will change."

"I know the kingdom is coming. But I cannot see how your Twelve can accomplish it. They are weak and divided. Does not your temple require righteous pillars? The house Jesus builds needs but the slightest breeze to bring it crashing down."

"Now, more than ever, Accuser, I need you. Do not fail me. Do not shrink from your testing, no matter the cost."

The Accuser straightened his back and shook his wings. "Never. I am yours."

"I know, my son. Now finish your accusations."

After the Crucifixion

The Accuser staggered into the portico outside the throne room. He had not waited for his legions to assemble. He did not see whether his compatriots had arrived. He took no notice of the Favored walking in small, aimless circles, nor did he note that the only light came from the Burning. The Burning did not chant, and the void of their voices swallowed the last of the Accuser's hopes.

The Accuser saw only that the great doors to the throne room were closed. The Incomparable stood at the doors, a stone-faced sentry, massive arms folded across his chest. The Accuser had not known the great doors could be closed; they never had been in the long eons of his existence. The Accuser half ran, half flew to the doors, only to be barred by the Incomparable's strong arm.

"The throne room is closed, Accuser."

"I have to see him, Incomparable. Get out of the way."

"The throne room is closed."

"Why are the doors closed?" he shouted. "Where is The Name? What is the meaning of this?"

"The throne room—"

Before the Incomparable could finish, the Strength crashed into the portico, lightning made flesh. His legions followed like a spring flood.

"Accuser!" he thundered. "What have you done?" His voice held no joy, no mirth, no trace of laughter. Only rage. In an instant he stood before them and grabbed the Accuser's robes. Effortlessly he threw the Accuser against the doors of the throne room. "How could you?"

The Accuser couldn't speak. He had witnessed the Strength's great fury—they all had—but he had never been the recipient, and it was fearsome indeed. As the Accuser struggled to marshal his thoughts, the Incomparable's massive hand fell on the Strength's shoulder.

"You forget yourself, Strength," the Incomparable said. "There will be no violence in this place. Not among our brothers."

The Strength turned his wild eyes up to the Incomparable's passive visage. "Have you not heard, Incomparable? Jesus is dead.

Dead. It was this one"—the Strength spat at the Accuser—"who arranged his death. He united Jesus' enemies against him. He enticed one of the Twelve to betray Jesus to them and another to flee his trial rather than give testimony. He ensured Pilate ignored his wife's vision. He persuaded the people of Jerusalem to call for his blood. At every turn, it was this scourge who enticed and plotted and schemed so that Jesus is even now being prepared for burial.

"Tell me, Accuser, Betrayer of your maker, God-killer—tell me why I should not pull my sword now and send you to the abyss to dwell with the unclean spirits?"

The Accuser stammered, mind still reeling. "I—I only did—The Name commanded—I did as I was instructed."

The Incomparable rumbled agreement. "We all heard that, Strength. The Name told him to test the Twelve, to test the leaders and the people of Jerusalem, to test Pilate. The Accuser did as his maker ordered. What of you?"

At that, the Strength sagged, releasing the Accuser and falling to his knees. He began to tear his robes in grief. "Every angel in my legion stood ready. Such a host has not been assembled since we sang of his birth. I prayed with him in the garden. I cheered when Simon attacked the guards. I followed him to his trial. When they began to beat him, I watched and waited for his command. As he was paraded through the streets, I walked every step with him, begging him to call on us. When they nailed him to the cross, when they raised him up, I and all my legions waited.

"I watched him die, all the while waiting for him to call us down." The Strength wept openly, and his grief rippled throughout the gathered legions, who all began to tear their robes and wail with him. Their grief touched even the Favored and the Burning, who finally raised their voices as well.

The Strength's condemnation rang in the Accuser's ears. "Betrayer of your maker. God-killer." He found himself shouting above the din of mourning. "I told him. I warned The Name that the humans could not be trusted." Someone tried to shush him, but he turned on his peers. "No. Listen to me. I will not shoulder this burden.

"You do not have to walk among them. You do not know their wickedness. Always when I condemn them, The Name makes excuses for them—insists I do not see the goodness in them. But there is no goodness left in them. Their sin has rotted them to the core. They deserve judgment. They deserve condemnation.

"The Name refused to heed me. Instead he became one of them, and he insisted I test them. So test them I did. I whispered in their ears, manipulated their desires, played on their fear. Even when they threatened Jesus himself, I did this because—unlike them—I will be what I was made to be. I will be faithful to The Name.

"You dare call me God-killer, Strength, you who stood by, sword in sheath, as he died? If I am guilty, so are you.

"But we are not the God-killers. It is them—his beloved humans. Do you think my tests were difficult? I assure you they were not. Do you think I had to whisper long to Caiaphas before he decided one life was worth the security of his people? Or to Pilate that no one would miss one more pretender king? They are all so filled with evil, they hardly need my help to find sin. They chase after it.

"How much better had The Name never formed Adam from the clay! How much better had Noah never built his ark, and humanity was washed from the earth! They to whom he shows endless mercy are the God-killers. They who break his covenants again and again are the betrayers of their maker."

The portico had fallen silent before his rage. The Accuser unfurled his wings. "Save your condemnations. I am a good son, a faithful servant."

With that, the Accuser fled the portico. He gave no thought to where he would go, but only to what he fled.

After the Ascension

The Accuser landed hard on the portico, and his legions swooped in, close and tight behind him. He stalked past the Healer and the Strength, ignoring their shouts of greeting. The doors stood wide open once more. So it was true.

The Favored again flew about the throne, chanting in counterpoint to the Burning below. The rainbow surrounding the throne gleamed brighter than ever, and the lightning and thunder crashed and rumbled. The Spirit's flame danced all around the throne, among the chanting hosts. The Name was seated on the throne. Jesus was there too, again, yet not as before. The Accuser recognized his human body, and even from there could see the wounds of his crucifixion marking his hands. Scars from thorns marked a halo on his head.

The Accuser marched toward the throne, so intent on his purpose he missed the legions upon legions; he did not hear their song. The Accuser did not kneel, but before he was even halfway to the throne, he found himself caught up as if for an audience. Suddenly he was in the midst of the throne, with The Name and the Lamb, the Spirit's fiery tongues dancing in circles around them.

They spoke as one, their voices a beautiful harmony. "Hail, Accuser! Where have you come from?" Their words stirred a love in the Accuser he quickly smothered beneath his mighty anger. He spat, "From roaming about on the earth. From circling it whole. I have brought a list of sinners who stand guilty before you."

"You have done well, my good and faithful servant, as always. I am proud of you."

The Accuser barely heard The Name's accolades. "Simon son of Jonah stands condemned. He disavowed you."

The Name smiled, and Jesus spoke. "There is no condemnation for Peter. I have forgiven him."

"James and John stand condemned. Andrew and Nathanael. Bartholomew. All the Twelve stand condemned. They abandoned you to death. They are faithless."

Jesus spoke again, his voice warm and kind. "There is no condemnation for the others. I have forgiven them."

"Caiaphas, high priest of Israel, stands condemned for conspiracy, collusion, and bearing false witness against the Messiah. Pilate, governor of Judea, emissary of Tiberius, Caesar of Rome, stands condemned for abuse of his position, for exploiting the poor, for idolatry. Herod Antipas stands condemned for taking the wife of his brother, for failing to keep the way of his people."

"There is no condemnation for Caiaphas, for Pilate or Antipas. They are all forgiven, Accuser."

"And what of Judas the Iscariot?" The Accuser was shouting now. "Is the one who betrayed you to death forgiven too?"

Sadness crept into Jesus' eyes, and he stepped toward the Accuser. "I wish Judas had not lost faith. His reconciliation would have been beautiful. But I do not condemn Judas. He too is forgiven. They are all forgiven, Accuser."

"You cannot do this."

At this, joy once again glowed through The Name's countenance, and his smile beamed. "Indeed. It is impossible to forgive humanity their sin. Their good fortune, then, that I am the Most High, who is not constrained by such small words as *possible* or *sin*. One sacrifice for all time. An infinite ransom redeemed. An invincible enemy run through with his own sword.

"It is finished, Accuser! Death has been defeated. All the powers of darkness converged on us and did their worst, and it was not enough. Even now, the world is being set right. Jesus is only the first fruits. Soon the whole of creation will be just as it was in the beginning. Remember those first days, when you were not Accuser, but Storyteller? Those days have come again. It is time for you to lay down condemnation."

The Name's mischievous joy fed the Accuser's rage. "Lay down condemnation?! From the first, the humans have gone their own way. They murder, rape, and oppress. They build palaces of sand that they might proclaim themselves kings of the brief moments they call life. How long after you gave them your Way did they wait to disobey you? Was it a month before Aaron fashioned an idol for them? How often did they beg to return to Egypt and put their chains back on themselves? How quickly did they forget their judges? How quickly did their kings rush into the arms of other gods? How many prophets did they murder?

"And when you came to them yourself, they abandoned you, denied you, schemed against you, crucified you. They want nothing to do with you. They are prodigal with your love. They waste your blessing. They ignore your provision. They are unworthy of your grace.

"Humanity stands before you condemned. Summon the Strength! Let the Incomparable lead the armies of heaven to avenge you. Let us show the world your power. Let us make you glorious!"

Jesus raised a hand to stop him. "Enough, Accuser. There is no condemnation. Those who stand in judgment are there because they choose darkness rather than light. But the gates will not be closed to them."

In all the millennia that the Accuser had stood in the midst of the throne, in the very presence of The Name, he had never tried to end the audience. But now he turned, leaned away from the throne, and in an instant stood near the doors again. The other archangels and their hosts had arrived, and he saw the Strength and the Healer whispering together behind the Incomparable, who strode to confront him.

The Accuser shouted to be heard over the harmonious chanting of the Favored and the Burning. "Do you know The Name's plan? To forgive humanity—they who destroyed his perfect creation, they who destroy each other daily! Do you know The Name would welcome them among us?"

The Incomparable gripped his arm, and the Accuser nearly winced. "Furl your wings, Accuser. We are all aware of what Jesus' resurrection means. He has ascended to the throne as Lord of a new creation." He squeezed harder, and now the Accuser did wince. "We are servants of The Name, as always."

The Accuser would not back down. "We are servants of the Most High. But tell me, Incomparable, what kind of god forswears vengeance on those who disregard his laws? What kind of god allows his enemies to crucify him? What kind of god forgives those enemies? For an eternity past we have served The Name faithfully, without wavering, without misstep. And what is our reward?"

The Incomparable's voice was iron. "Our reward is to serve The Name, to abide in his love for us and ours for him. As it has always been, so shall it always be. It is enough."

"Do you not listen? The Name would forgive humanity. The Name would welcome into his presence those who have no regard for his Way. He would have them join us. We who serve. We who remain faithful. We who watch. But tell me: What do we see?

"I will tell you what I see. I, the Accuser, who was tasked in Eden to walk among Adam's children and record their failings—I offer no succor, Healer. I do not defend the innocent, Strength. I do not stand in heaven, Incomparable. I walk in the mud. I note each sin, every misstep. I hear every lie. I record every broken vow. I describe every murder, every rape. I see each act of oppression, each abuse of power.

"No one knows the wickedness of humanity as I do. They do not deserve forgiveness. They deserve what The Name himself tasked me to dispense: condemnation, judgment, justice."

The Incomparable cut him off. "You forget yourself, Accuser. You are to accuse no more. Once they stand condemned, it is for The Name to dispense justice as he sees fit."

The Accuser shook free and shouted to the whole throne room, "This is not justice. The Name allows them to trample his holiness in the dirt, to put it on a cross and destroy it. Now he would welcome them among us as equals? No, as more than equals, as favored sons and daughters! Will you kneel to them, Incomparable? What of you, Strength?

"Will you bow and scrape and serve they who prove their unworthiness with every breath? Will you serve the very creatures who would tear down heaven and crucify their creator? I will not." The Accuser swept his arm to encompass the great throne room of heaven. "I will not allow The Name to destroy all this for the sake of his love for these rebellious children."

The Incomparable squared his stance. "You will not allow?" His voice had a sharp edge.

The Accuser turned toward the throne. "The Name stands condemned. His love for humanity betrays us all." He drew his sword. "To me, my legion!"

The Accuser charged the throne, his hosts at his back.

> And war broke out in heaven; Michael and his angels fought against the dragon. The dragon and his angels fought back, but they were defeated, and there was no longer any place for them in heaven. . . .
>
> Rejoice then, you heavens
>   and those who dwell in them!
> But woe to the earth and the sea,
>   for the devil has come down to you
> with great wrath,
>   because he knows that his time is short!
> (Revelation 12:7-8, 12)

14

RUNNING WITH THE DEVIL

On Devils, Older Brothers, and Pharisees Then and Now

To be an older brother is to live in a near-constant state of righteous indignation. Once when I was around thirteen years old, I was watching TV on the couch. For reasons clear only to the inscrutable logic of younger siblings, my younger brother entered the living room and stood directly between me and the TV, facing me with a mischievous smile. Not one to escalate a sibling disagreement unnecessarily—especially with a parent in the house—I offered a kind, measured response. "Please move."

My brother stood silent, his Cheshire smile unchanged.

"Please move. You're blocking my view."

Silence. His smile mocked me.

"Okay. I'm going to count to five. If you haven't moved, I'm going to punch you." I had exhausted all peaceful options in my adolescent brain. It was time to go nuclear.

"One." His posture didn't even shift.

"Two." Was that a glint in his eye?

"Three." What is his game here?

"Four." He must *want* to get punched. How else to explain this?[1]

I let out a deep sigh. This was going to hurt him a lot more than it hurt me. "Five."

I stood up, walked toward him, and punched him in the stomach. Immediately he let out a bloodcurdling shriek that brought my mom running from whatever she was doing. Of course, I was punished while my brother escaped with nothing more than an exasperated warning.

Elder siblings struggle with grace. We love it when we're on the receiving end, but it's difficult to convince us that grace is evenly distributed in a household with younger siblings. It's not so different in the church, where older—and allegedly more mature—Christians often struggle to celebrate when those new to the church or those outside the church receive grace. As a result, too often we are grumpy, cruel, or disenchanted with our own faith. We drift far from our first love and the white-hot passion of the grace that saved us.

Can an elder sibling be convinced that grace is a good thing? This is the question Satan invites us to ask.

The Devil's (Not) in the Details

I was speaking with a group of pastors once about how to do outreach for young people. We were discussing the merits of bringing in a contemporary worship band for a concert. In response, one of the pastors asked, "If rock music summons demons, why should I have a rock band in my church?"

Fortunately I am the product of an evangelical youth group from the early nineties, so this was not my first exposure to the idea that rock music is satanic. The pastor's question stemmed from an iteration of Satan's origin story, specifically that the being we now call Satan, Lucifer, and the devil was once the worship leader of heaven. Now that he has fallen, it stands to reason that he uses music to corrupt humanity. And bands like AC/DC, Queen, and Kansas use album art, lyrics, and backmasking to heighten the demonic activity initiated by beat of the rock 'n' roll.[2]

Musical conspiracy theories aside, most beats of what I will call the Lucifer myth are familiar: Lucifer was an archangel who decided he should rule heaven instead of God. He waged war and was cast out of heaven into hell. Now he is the devil, also called Satan, who tempts humanity to lead as many away from God as possible.

The problem is that big pieces of this story—including the name Lucifer—aren't anywhere in the Bible. Other important statements about Satan that *are* in the Bible—including the timeline of his fall—are ignored. If we start with what the Bible explicitly says about Satan, a different picture emerges. Spoiler alert: it doesn't have much to do with rock music.

Versions of the Lucifer myth as outlined above are recognizable as early as Origen, a church father who lived in Alexandria, Egypt, around 200 CE. The Alexandrian fathers popularized allegorical biblical interpretation. We could spend pages on allegorical interpretation, but it suffices to say the Alexandrian fathers did not concern themselves with historical context.

Origen identified the devil as the serpent in Genesis—one of the first Christian writers to do so. He also identified the devil as the angel of death in Egypt, Azazel in Leviticus 16, and Satan in Job. Origen's identification of both the prince of Babylon in Isaiah 14 and the king of Tyre in Ezekiel 28 have become the cornerstone texts for the Lucifer myth, along with Revelation 12.[3] Careful readings of these passages illuminates where various pieces of the Lucifer myth originated and why using them to talk about Satan should give us pause.[4]

The name Lucifer comes to us from Isaiah 14. The prophet is speaking against the prince of Babylon, whom he identifies as the

"Day Star" and "son of Dawn." The Day Star is the planet Venus, which often appears at dawn and is the brightest object in the sky other than the sun and moon. When Jerome translated Isaiah into Latin, he rendered "Day Star" as the Latin word *Lucifer*, which means "light-bringer." The translators of the King James Version worked not from Greek and Hebrew texts, but from the Latin. The translators left the word *Lucifer* in the text, treating it as a proper name, so the devil got a new name.

This son of Dawn was thought to ascend to heaven to rule in God's place but instead has been cast down into "the Pit." It sure *sounds* like the Lucifer story, but the prophet is using poetic language to describe the Babylonian Empire's arrogance. Without already assuming the Lucifer myth, it's not immediately obvious that Isaiah 14 has anything to do with Satan. Though some church fathers, following Origen's lead, choose to read the prophecy as multilayered, many others, including both Luther and Calvin, are adamant that the passage has nothing to do with the devil.[5]

The same is true of the other passage popularly assumed to inform Lucifer's story, Ezekiel 28:12-19. Using typological language that would have been familiar to the ears of his listeners, Ezekiel cast another monarch—the king of Tyre—as Adam walking in Eden. Like our first father, this king proved unfaithful and therefore deserving of the judgment God unleashed. Again, there is no supernatural being. Ezekiel does at least feature primordial history, but Adam in Eden is typological language utilized to comment on a contemporary figure. No devil here either.[6]

The clearest accounting of Satan's fall is Revelation 12:7-9:

> And war broke out in heaven; Michael and his angels fought against the dragon. The dragon and his angels fought back, but they were defeated, and there was no longer any place

> for them in heaven. The great dragon was thrown down, that ancient serpent, who is called the Devil and Satan, the deceiver of the whole world—he was thrown down to the earth, and his angels were thrown down with him.

Here Satan is pictured as a dragon, called "that ancient serpent" and "the Devil."[7] And there is a war in heaven. Satan even takes a third of the angels with him when he's cast down.

But *when* did this happen? Did it really happen before the earth was created, as the Lucifer story insists? Not according to Revelation 12. The first six verses tell the story of a woman who is both Mary and Israel—she is crowned with twelve stars—who gives birth to a son. Lest we're confused as to the identity of this child, the Revelator attaches a messianic psalm to his birth. This is Jesus.

The dragon threatened Jesus, but before it could consume him, Jesus was "snatched away and taken to God and to his throne" (Revelation 12:5). The whole of Jesus' incarnation, death, and resurrection is wrapped up in the space between words. Jesus was born, and then he was caught up into heaven.

And *then* the war broke out. According to Revelation, Satan's war was triggered by Jesus' ascension to the throne of heaven. (More on this in a moment.)

Part of our struggle is that we want human answers to cosmic questions.[8] Revelation, for instance, is not a biography of Satan. It is about the seven churches of Asia remaining faithful to God in the midst of an unfaithful culture. The Revelator arranges Satan's story (and his relationship to Rome) specifically to serve that purpose.

None of the texts that inform the Lucifer myth tell the story of an angel who rebelled against God before creation began. The only way to find that story in the Bible is to go looking for it—and to read verses out of context. Fortunately the Bible does talk about

Satan. But if we focus on what the Bible *does* say, a different picture emerges.

Law and Order: Heaven

There are only three references to Satan in the Old Testament, and the first is not in Genesis. Though many readers assume the talking serpent in Genesis 3 is the devil incarnate, Genesis itself treats the animal not as a divine being but as a talking animal.[9]

Lucifer does not appear at all, and the word *devil* is not used until the New Testament. The Old Testament is rife with demons and pagan gods, but there is no chief fallen angel. We do find, however, a figure named Satan, who appears in the early chapters of Job, Zechariah, and—most troubling—in 1 Chronicles. Satan is a Hebrew word that means "accuser."[10] This is a title, a role fulfilled in ancient Near Eastern royal courts and roughly analogous to our prosecuting attorney today. The accuser represented the state (that is, the king) in legal proceedings. With that in mind (and leaving the Lucifer myth out of it), these three texts offer a very different picture of Satan's identity and role.

1 Chronicles. "Satan stood up against Israel, and incited David to count the people of Israel" (1 Chronicles 21:1). This text seems pretty straightforward. Satan incited David to sin, which is exactly what we expect from Satan. The problem is that both books of Chronicles are a recap of the story of Israel found in 1 Samuel through 2 Kings. The original version of this story is in 2 Samuel 24. Brace yourself; it's a little bit different: "The anger of the Lord was kindled against Israel, and he incited David against them, saying, 'Go, count the people of Israel and Judah'" (2 Samuel 24:1).

In the original version of the story, it's not Satan but God who incited David to sin. When the author of Chronicles retold the story, he changed God to Satan. That's quite an oversight. It's one thing to mix up Hitler and Stalin and something else to confuse either of them with Mother Teresa. (How did his editor not catch that?)

There is another possibility: that the author of Chronicles did not see Satan as an adversary of God but as a functionary of God's divine court. If Satan worked for God, so to speak, and if Satan were responsible for testing humanity on behalf of God, then 1 Chronicles could be true, because Satan tested David. *And* 2 Samuel could be true, because as divine king, God is ultimately responsible for the actions of the divine court.

Zechariah and Job. In Zechariah 3, the prophet receives a vision of Joshua, the high priest of Israel. The vision is one of redemption:

> Then he showed me the high priest Joshua standing before the angel of the LORD, and Satan standing at his right hand to accuse him. And the LORD said to Satan, "The LORD rebuke you, O Satan! The LORD who has chosen Jerusalem rebuke you! Is not this man a brand plucked from the fire?" Now Joshua was dressed with filthy clothes as he stood before the angel. The angel said to those who were standing before him, "Take off his filthy clothes." And to him he said, "See, I have taken your guilt away from you, and I will clothe you with festal apparel." (Zechariah 3:1-4)

Here Satan is fulfilling the role of the accuser. He stands in the heavenly court, ready to declare Joshua's guilt—and by extension all of Israel. But instead God rebukes him—and God offers forgiveness and redemption instead.

I had never read either 1 Chronicles nor Zechariah until I was in Bible college. But I had heard Job's story often as a teen, and

Satan's appearance in the book was always difficult to reconcile with the Lucifer myth:

> One day the heavenly beings came to present themselves before the Lord, and Satan also came among them. The Lord said to Satan, "Where have you come from?" Satan answered the Lord, "From going to and fro on the earth, and from walking up and down on it."
>
> The Lord said to Satan, "Have you considered my servant Job? There is no one like him on the earth, a blameless and upright man who fears God and turns away from evil." Then Satan answered the Lord, "Does Job fear God for nothing? Have you not put a fence around him and his house and all that he has, on every side? You have blessed the work of his hands, and his possessions have increased in the land. But stretch out your hand now, and touch all that he has, and he will curse you to your face."
>
> The Lord said to Satan, "Very well, all that he has is in your power; only do not stretch out your hand against him!" So Satan went out from the presence of the Lord. (Job 1:6-12)

In Job, Satan is presented as a member of the heavenly court. His role is scouring the earth, recording the sins of humanity, and reporting them to God. The conflict in Job—at least in heaven—is because Satan is unconvinced that Job's faithfulness to God is earnest. In Satan's eyes, Job is untested. God allows Satan to test Job, to prove his faithfulness.

Again this story is problematic if Satan and God are already adversaries. But if Satan is a functionary of heaven, his presence in the heavenly court makes sense.[11]

The Accuser Is Thrown Down

What about Satan in the New Testament? We get echoes of the Old Testament accuser as we hear Jesus warn Peter that Satan wanted to sift the disciples like wheat (Luke 22:31-32), implying a testing to see who is truly faithful. And even Jesus' wilderness temptation can be read in light of Job; could it not be that Satan tested Jesus' faithfulness to see whether he was in fact fit to be Israel's Messiah?

But elsewhere Satan is the devil, a word in Greek that means "deceiver." He is called a roaring lion (1 Peter 5:8), one who has sinned from the beginning (1 John 3:8-10), a schemer (Ephesians 6:11), a murderer from the beginning who has no truth in him (John 8:44), and one who has the power of death (Hebrews 2:14).

What happened between the Old and New Testaments? How did Satan go from divinely appointed prosecutor to deceiver and liar? The short answer is this: Jesus was raised from the dead and ascended to the throne of heaven.

All the books that comprise what we now call the New Testament were written at least a generation after Jesus was raised from the dead. They are shaped by decades of reflection by the new Christian community on the meaning of Jesus' incarnation, death, and resurrection. And most of the New Testament writers were Jewish, drawing on the long Jewish tradition that includes on the periphery the figure of the accuser.

Again and again, the New Testament writers insist that something fundamental changed in the cosmos when Jesus was raised from the dead. By dying, he defeated the powers of sin and death. By rising from the dead, he proved that God's way leads to life—even if God must resurrect to make it so. In the wake of Jesus' resurrection, there is no longer a need for an accuser. In raising Jesus from the dead, God no longer counts our trespasses against us, as Paul observed in 2 Corinthians 5:19, and as he says in Romans 8:1-2: "There is therefore now no condemnation for those who are in Christ Jesus. For the law of the Spirit of life in Christ Jesus has set you free from the law of sin and of death."

The book of Revelation tells us that when Jesus ascended to heaven, when his work of rescue was completed, Satan went to war. He was cast down, of course, but that's not quite the end of the story. Revelation tells us,

> Rejoice then, you heavens
>   and those who dwell in them!
> But woe to the earth and the sea,
>   for the devil has come down to you
> with great wrath,
>   because he knows that his time is short!" (12:12)

In the wake of the war in heaven, Satan was cast down to the earth. He knew his time was short, so he embarked on a mission: to take as many people with him as he could. But how? Death cannot stop the God who raises the dead. So how would the dragon make war on the throne?

Revelation tells us he is the deceiver, the devil. Satan's weapon is lies—a theme that runs throughout the New Testament. The Satan of the Old Testament, God's accuser, was anything *but* a liar. He reported the sin of humanity that they might stand justly convicted before God. But now that there *is no condemnation*, Satan can only lie.

Revelation goes on to tell us that Satan set out specifically to make war on the people of God, to deceive us into idolatry and faithlessness. Satan convinces us, like Cain, to ground our identity in temporal, temporary things rather than in the eternal love of God. Satan whispers in our ears that, like Samson, we should satisfy every craving and take whatever our eyes find desirable, so that we cease to be God's holy people. Satan teaches us to be afraid so that, like Jezebel, we look to false gods for safety and security.

Satan convinces us that if we work hard enough, we can make everyone happy so that, like Herod, we overlook and devalue the most vulnerable among us. Satan blinds us to the rot in our family trees so that, like Herodias, we perpetuate the sins of our ancestors. And Satan tells us stories of a god who wins, a god of victory and conquest, so that, like Judas, we cannot hear the voice of the crucified one.

Lie after lie after lie—all were designed to distract us from the power of the Spirit at work in us to bring new life.[12]

No wonder, then, that by the time Christians were writing, Satan had become for them an eternal evil, someone rotten from the beginning. John the Revelator embodied him as a fearsome multiheaded sea serpent. For him, Satan was the Leviathan of ancient Near Eastern mythology that lurked in the depths of the seas, the embodiment of the chaotic forces of anticreation. Satan was the antithesis of God's life-giving power.

All of this is because Jesus' resurrection eliminated the need for an accuser. Satan is not the heavenly worship leader exiled from heaven before the creation of the world. So he is someone who's basically mad that he's out of a job. That sounds silly, but could it be the most insidious evil?

Aggravating Grace (That Saved a Wretch Like Me)

Satan found God's grace so offensive that he went to war with the Creator. Unfortunately Satan's attitude is common. Jesus encountered it again and again, particularly among the religious of his day. During his ministry, he developed a reputation as a friend of sinners. He was apparently quite the party animal, because rumors swirled that he was a glutton and a drunkard.[13] Again and again, the religious leaders of Jesus' day were scandalized that a respectable rabbi like him would be caught dead with the likes of the sinners he hung around.

Luke wrote, "All the tax collectors and sinners were coming near to listen to him. And the Pharisees and the scribes were grumbling and saying, 'This fellow welcomes sinners and eats with them'" (Luke 15:1-2). In response, Jesus told three parables to illustrate why he was where he was—at a very public feast with sinners. The first is about a shepherd who loses one sheep out of a hundred and leaves the ninety-nine to search for the one lost. Jesus said there's a bigger party in heaven when one sinner repents than when ninety-nine righteous people persist in their faithfulness.

The second is about a woman who loses one coin out of ten. When she finds the missing money, she throws a party for her village.

The third story, which is commonly called the parable of the prodigal son, features a father and two sons. The younger demands his inheritance, flees, squanders it, and returns home groveling, only to be met by his father with open arms. The father even throws a party.

Jesus really liked parties.

This story doesn't end with a party, however. It ends out in the fields, where the older brother is working and refusing to come to the party. The father pleads with him to come, but the son replies, "For all these years I have been working like a slave for you, and I have never disobeyed your command; yet you have never given me even a young goat so that I might celebrate with my friends. But when this son of yours came back, who has devoured your property with prostitutes, you killed the fatted calf for him" (Luke 15:29-30).

The older brother refused to be under the same roof with a long-lost son who had been welcomed home. And Jesus compared the religious leaders to this older brother. He said that if they knew God as well as they claimed, they would be right where he was—in the midst of the sinners and tax collectors.

Instead the Pharisees' religion had made them bitter and angry. Somehow their zeal for God had led them *away* from reflecting God's character. Rather than rejoicing that God's wayward children had come home to find forgiveness and reconciliation, they got angry. They went to war with Jesus, much like Satan went to war with God.

At stake is a fundamental misunderstanding of God's character—or an outright rejection of it. If Jesus' characterization of the Pharisees in the person of the older brother is accurate, they are blinded by scarcity. The younger brother took his inheritance, which means the father's reply—"All that is mine is yours"—is literally true. The father was using the older brother's property to throw the welcome-home party. What good can come from wasting resources on a son who's already wasted so much?

But grace is not a limited good. God is infinite and unbound, the very Creator of the universe. God cannot run out of grace.

The older brother had a legitimate complaint. It wasn't fair, in his eyes, that the younger brother got to waste his father's property and then come back and all was forgiven. One brother never sins and one does nothing but sin, yet in the end, both receive the same reward. It's profoundly unfair, and we might excuse the Pharisees' anger. Again and again, the prophets of Israel raged against injustice. Again and again, they insisted that God will reward the righteous and punish the wicked.

But the Pharisees forgot how the prophets described God again and again. As Jesus reminded them in another showdown over the same issue (a dispute over the call of Matthew the tax collector), "Those who are well have no need of a physician, but those who are sick. Go and learn what this means, 'I desire mercy, not sacrifice.' For I have come to call not the righteous but sinners" (Matthew 9:12-13).

Jesus was quoting the prophet Hosea, pointing out to the Pharisees that their view of God's justice was skewed. Yes, God is just. And yes, God punishes the wicked. But God is *slow* to anger and *quick* to show mercy. And what God is most interested in from God's people is *not* slavish adherence to rules. That's the sacrificial system embodied in the myopic concern for justice we see in the Pharisees.

Jesus reminded them that to be like God is to rush to show mercy and to celebrate when sinners repent and find life. That's supposed to be *good news*, and it's worth throwing a party for.

Perhaps the most disturbing aspect of this graceless attitude we see in the older brother, in the Pharisees, and in Satan is a conviction that they are not living the best life. The older brother complained that he had been working like a slave while his brother went off and lived it up. You don't have to hang around too many church folks before the Pharisees' attitude rings true. Frankly, a lot of religious people view a religious life as a sacrifice. Sinners get to have all the fun—sex, drugs, rock 'n' roll—while the religious folks sacrifice fun, joy, and excitement for an eternal reward. As a fringe benefit, we've decided we get to sit in judgment over the sinners, and it's not long before a certain smug self-satisfaction creeps in as we contemplate their eternal torment.[14] *Have all the fun you want now. We'll see who's laughing for eternity!* No wonder the religious folks get upset when God shows up. Rather than standing aloof and apart in judgment with them, God is partying with the sinners.

Behind all of this is the conviction that to serve God is to work like a slave and that the life God calls us into isn't good, isn't fun, isn't life. This simply isn't what we see in Jesus. Everyone wanted to be around him. Wherever he went, people found life, a life that was so attractive they left the patterns of sin they'd been living to follow him. So many of God's children who had been prodigal with God's grace found in Jesus something better than they had known in their sin.

No wonder they called it good news. No wonder they wanted to be with him.

It should bother us that our churches are full mainly of Christians. We should lose sleep over the fact that most pastors don't have significant relationships with people outside the church, let alone those the church typically derides as sinners. If your faith has turned you into a boring, joyless stick-in-the-mud, there's something wrong with your faith.

Christians who refuse to extend God's grace to the world around them are truly satanic. Maybe we can't believe grace is free, or we think we've earned more than someone else, or we're simply not convinced life with God is the excessive, overflowing, abundant life Jesus promised. In any case, our sinful picture of God poisons our relationships with our neighbors.

But when a church gets this right, it's life changing.

I knew I wanted to be a part of Catalyst Church from the moment I heard about the chairs. The church had just lost its lead pastor and had gotten my name through the grapevine. I was on the phone with the other staff pastor, and I asked him to tell me about the church. He said, "We're a church that's for all the people who aren't here yet."

He then told me a story that began shortly after they had moved into their building. They were a small congregation, but as part of moving into the building, they had ensured they had enough chairs for the time being. Their pastor, Levi, knew they would need more if they were going to grow. But being a small, young church that had just moved into a new building, they didn't have much extra cash.

Levi took it to the people. He reminded them that Catalyst had always been a church for people who don't like church—people who have been burned in the past or can't connect with God through the more traditional forms of worship in which they had been raised. He called them to picture the people in the community surrounding their new building, and he pointed out that there was literally no place for those people in the new building. They had enough chairs for themselves, but not for anyone else.

The congregation dug deep and quickly raised the money for all those extra chairs. And sure enough, the chairs weren't extra chairs for long. More and more people discovered a church that was for them, a place that welcomed them as they were and gave them the space—and the grace—to learn to trust the Spirit to make them new.

Catalyst is a party thrown by a father who's overjoyed that his prodigal children have come home. We've got plenty of prodigals, and we've got plenty of older brothers too. Many of them thought for way too long that religion was all about arbitrary rules handed down by a distant God. They had spent their lives working like slaves, and now they're slowly realizing they're not slaves but children, invited to the party.

God's party has enough chairs for everyone.

The older brothers among us need healing as much as the prodigals in our midst. The antidote is to listen to the voice of the God who stands pleading with us in the field. We must reconnect with our first love, the Jesus we meet in the Gospels who came to announce good news, to topple the powerful from their thrones, and to lift up the outcast and oppressed. The God who was proud to associate with prostitutes, tax collectors, and sinners, because they were finding life in him. The God who allowed himself to be interrupted by children and the chronically ill and Roman centurions.

For our churches to become hospitals for sinners rather than country clubs for saints, we need a good dose of humility, realizing that we're all sinners in need of grace. Spiritual pratices such as confessing our sin to each other or daily prayers of examen can help us to remember that all we do is through God's grace.

Our churches must quit hiding in our sanctuaries. If we are the body of Christ, we must go where we know Christ's body went when he was incarnate among us.

The sin of Satan is refusing to extend grace to the world around us. Receiving grace is easy. Extending that same grace to others isn't easy. We must remain in the Spirit to allow the Spirit to cultivate in us the fruit of love, joy, peace, and patience. As we are transformed more and more into God's image, we become more graceful as God is graceful. We rediscover the joy of sinners turning from their sins to find life. And we realize that's something to celebrate.

EPILOGUE

EMPATHY FOR THE DEVIL

What to Do When It Turns Out You're the Villain

The summer after my junior year in college, I worked for the grounds crew at my university. It was miserable work, but several of my friends were on the crew, so we had fun despite the long hours and summer heat. Our boss quickly noticed we were hard workers, and he noticed the other crew was lazy. While we mowed fields and edged dormitory sidewalks, the other crew parked their truck outside a classroom building and sat in the air-conditioned lobby.

We could tell our boss knew what the other crew was up to, because he started assigning our crew all the hardest and most important jobs. We were furious. Why didn't he fire them or at least discipline them? Days stretched into weeks, and nothing improved—least of all our workload.

A deep hatred grew in my spirit for my boss. Okay, it didn't just grow. I *cultivated* it. I fantasized about telling him off all the time—even when I wasn't at work. I became consumed by how much I hated him. When I finally noticed how toxic my attitude had become, I began praying both that God would change him and that God would help me deal with my anger.

Over the next week, something strange happened: I learned several pieces of information about my boss that gave me insight into his personal and professional life. Nothing major—no scandals, nothing earth-shattering. But those few pieces of information transformed how I saw him. Suddenly I understood where he was coming from. I still didn't agree—far from it. But I found I couldn't be angry with him anymore. In fact, I found myself wanting to work harder, to do what I could to take stress off his plate.

Nothing changed that summer—except my perception of my boss. A little empathy changed me.

There's no such thing as monsters.[1] When we look across the aisle or across the city or across the world and declare others to be monsters, there's no surer sign we've misunderstood them. My favorite of the glut of young-adult, postapocalyptic novels is the *Pure* trilogy by Julianna Baggott. We interviewed her on the StoryMen podcast about the process of writing, and she spoke specifically about one of the series' most popular characters, El Capitan:

> I really wanted El Capitan to be a bad guy. When I really dwelled in his existence . . . he could no longer be a bad guy. . . . When you look at someone's full humanity, what they truly fear, what they truly desire, what they've been through, you can't help but know them. And once you know them, forgiveness is just a breath away.[2]

We make villains out of what we don't understand. We insist they could never be like us. But a closer examination reveals we are separated by degrees, not kind. We all have the same sickness. Evil queens and femme fatales, murderous brothers and crazy kings, betrayers and devils live among us—and they are us.

I hope this journey through the lives of some of the Bible's most infamous villains has been as surprising and enjoyable for you as writing it was for me. Again and again as I dwelled in the existences of these devils, I found Baggott's words to be true. The more of their humanity I saw, the easier it was to understand them, to hurt for them, to feel compassion and love. I found myself rooting for them, even though I knew their stories ended in tragedy. I found myself heartbroken rather than angry or self-righteous.

Most of all, I found myself in these villains. I saw how easily I could become them and how I was often already following in their footsteps. These are the great gifts of empathy: compassion and understanding.

We desperately need empathy in our world today. The next time you come across someone you don't understand, ask why before you rush to judgment. When others reveal themselves to be monsters (and therefore a threat to *you*), remember *they* are just like *you*. They bear the image of God. They love someone. They are hurt. Remember they have walked a path to get to where they are, just like you have walked a path to get to where you are.

May this journey into the hearts of the Bible's worst villains ultimately give you a clearer picture of the God in whose image both you and they are made. May we all be quicker to listen and slower to speak. Let us rush to show mercy and be slow to anger. Let us learn to see the full humanity of the other. And as we see, may the Spirit grant understanding, that we may find forgiveness just a breath away.

As we learn to see the villains lurking within ourselves, may the Spirit breathe new life into us. As we become whole, may we become a people able to love even the devils we meet and to find them transformed into friends by that love.

ACKNOWLEDGMENTS

First and foremost, to my wife, Amanda. *Usted me ha apoyado en cada paso del camino, y siempre supo que este libro iba a existir. ¡Te quiero hasta la luna y más allá! Vamos a bucear con tiburones para celebrar! Además, ¿es esto correcto? Probablemente no. Utilicé el traductor de google.*

To the StoryMen, Clay Morgan and Matt Mikalatos. This book would definitely not exist without you. You coached and prodded me every step along the way, letting me bounce ideas off you, reading drafts, and celebrating with me. I can't wait to see what's next for us.

To my agent, David van Diest, who thinks I'm a better writer than I actually am and proved it by pulling this idea out of me.

To my editor, Al Hsu, who tolerated frantic emails and phone calls, and who made this book several factors of ten better than what I turned in to him initially. You're a wizard, sir, and this Slytherin has nothing but respect for your Ravenclaw awesomeness.

To my best friend, Tom Fuerst. This book has your fingerprints all over it. No one else has so shaped how I understand God and how I pastor.

To My Awesome Podcasting Cohosts

Bryne Lewis, thank you for always pushing me to think more deeply and clearly. We need to karaoke again, obviously.

Tara Thomas Smith and Heather Gerbsch Daugherty, you've been huge encouragements since day one. I'm thankful to think theologically with you. You make me a better pastor, and I can only hope the converse is true to some degree.

Mo Zahedi and Stacey Silverii, thank you both for reading and giving me honest feedback and insight. There's definitely no one else I'd rather explore an abandoned cabin in the woods with—especially because I'm pretty sure I'm faster than Mo at least.

Elizabeth Glass Turner, your perspective and insight are endlessly fascinating. Thank you for your honesty, wisdom, and vulnerability.

To My Beta Readers, Who Gave Me Encouragement and Insight

Lorie Langdon (check out her books; they're awesome!), Blake Atwood, Guy Decalmbre, Sara Kay Ndjerareou (they all have books; check them too), Jennifer Cho, Darryl Schafer, Tim Brooks, Amy Dennis, Abby Walls, Elijah Bender, Mikey Fissel (of the Reel World Theology podcast), and Jonathan Sprang, your insights and encouragement have been invaluable.

Tom Oord, you are one of the kindest and most generous people I've ever encountered. I pray one day I live out my theology half as well as you live out yours.

Da MAC, thank you for sharing in this journey with me and for letting me be part of yours. I'm so proud to support your dreams. Thank you for supporting mine.

Marissa Decalmbre and the whole Art House Dallas community, it is a rare privilege to create with you. Special thanks to my incredible Art House Dallas writers' group, Rachel, Baily, Amber, Ryan, Amanda, and Julia, who have been a constant support and encouragement. Thank you for reading, critiquing, and cheering.

Ashley Williams, thanks for your friendship and wisdom in getting the book launched into the world.

Wendell Simpson, thank you for your wisdom, insight, and encouragement.

Paul and Jamie Kepner, thanks for the excellent book trailer.

To the Artists Who Put Skin on My Characters

Lars VanZandt (he's also our tattoo artist; check out his stuff), you're one of my oldest friends and a constant encouragement. Thank you for sharing your art with this project.

The always amazing M. S. Corley—I'm glad our love of horror brought us together.

Tye-rannosaurus Wrecks Lombardi, is there anything you're not awesome at? Thank you for being my friend.

Katie Fisher, I find your skill, insight, and creativity challenging and inspiring.

J. Todd Anderson, your artistic vision has long inspired me. I am humbled and proud that you agreed to be part of this project.

And to My Community, Near and Far[1]

My amazing Catalyst Church family, thank you for giving me the space to write this book *and* the space to explore these ideas. You are an incredibly special congregation, and I can never quite believe I have the privilege to be your pastor.

My leadership team—Tim and Pam Moriarty, Doug Booth, John Hewitt, and Brenda Spencer—you made this book possible. Thank you for your love, encouragement, and support.

My preaching team—Sue Sweeney, Tim Basselin, Tommy Cash, Joshua Morris, Debbie Reese, and Amy Dennis—you teach me so much, and I'm honored to minister with you.

Beavercreek Nazarene congregation, I've been gone a little over three years, but it seems like yesterday. Thank you for giving me space to work out a lot of the material that ended up in this book.

My housemates, Jeff and Sue, Stella, and Clara, thanks for putting up with me holed up many evenings as I wrote and blasted music.

Michael Hughes, you listened to a *lot* of complaining about my process of bringing this book into the world—and a lot of complaining about triceps. Thank you for your friendship and encouragement.

Jesse Clark (AKA the King of Dayton), I know you were already a fan of these characters, since they're the bad guys. I hope this book helps you connect with all the folks who live north of four. I'm so glad our initial suspicion of each other transformed quickly into a lifelong brotherhood.

My family, which has shaped me and let me write about you, I hope by this point in the book you still claim me. Rich and Kerry Morrell, Marshall and Jan Madill, Rick and Lois Kohnen, thank you for love, support, and encouragement. Corrie and Rusty House, Aaron and Alison Madill, Brandon and Amanda Kohnen, Mike and Lindsey Morrell, Jenni Morrell, and Heather and Scott Souther, I have more wonderful siblings and in-laws than anyone should reasonably expect in one lifetime. Laurice Madill, thanks for showing me what it looks like to always have an open door and a hot meal ready.

My grandmother, Helen Barnes, you showed me what empathy looks like when I didn't have a clue. Thank you for your constant, faithful witness. I don't think this book would exist without you.

Keven Wentworth, JC and Sheila Slone, Anthony and Leah Mako, Jonathan Odom, and Ty Walls, thank you for incubating these ideas, challenging me, and loving me.

Kathleen Morgason, not only did you send me to the principal, you also saw something worth cultivating in that clueless sixteen-year-old kid.

The awesome team at InterVarsity Press, you're the textbook definition of "above and beyond."

I wrote a lot of this book at the Book Club Café, Opening Bell Coffee Shop, and the Pearl Cup. Thanks for letting me hang out, drink excellent coffee, and write my heart out.

I hope it's not a cliché to thank *you*, the reader. This book has a lot of challenging stuff in it, and if you made it this far, it means a lot to me. The process of cutting myself open and pouring it all out onto the page—then having you read it—well, it's scary and exhilarating all at once. I hope you've found the reading of it life giving. I pray you've heard the Spirit whispering to you in these pages.

NOTES

Introduction

[1]The showers at Dachau were created and perfected at other camps. Though they were installed at Dachau, the camp was liberated before they could be used.

[2]"Ein Konzentrationslager fur politische Gefangene," *Munchner Neueste Nachrichten*, March 21, 1933, 1.

[3]"Timeline of Dachau," Jewish Virtual Library, www.jewishvirtuallibrary .org/timeline-of-dachau. Accessed February 24, 2017.

2 You Wouldn't Like Me When I'm Angry

[1]Andy Crouch, *Playing God: Redeeming the Gift of Power* (Downers Grove, IL: InterVarsity Press, 2014), 55.

[2]Like Cain, many of us inherit our identities from others—particularly our families. We'll address this when we reach Herodias.

[3]Stephen A. Diamond, "The Primacy of Anger Problems," *Psychology Today*, January 18, 2009, www.psychologytoday.com/blog/evil-deeds /200901/the-primacy-anger-problems.

[4]Cain's inability to understand affected his relationship with God as well as his neighbor. As theologian Miroslav Volf reminds us, pride disrupts our praise of God and therefore our sense of who we really are: "God doesn't need our praise to be God or to 'feel' like God; we need to praise God to be truly ourselves—creatures made in the image of God." Miroslav Volf, *Exclusion and Embrace: A Theological Exploration of Identity, Otherness, and Reconciliation* (Nashville, TN: Abingdon, 1996), 95.

4 I'm Not Like Everybody Else

[1]Interpreters as early as Pseudo-Philo—a rough contemporary of Jesus—focus on Samson as the true villain of the story, as does Judges itself. Josey Bridges Snyder, "Delilah and Her Interpreters," in *Women's Bible Commentary*, 3rd ed., ed. Carol A. Newsom (Louisville, KY: John Knox, 2012), 138-42.

[2]See Melissa Jackson's excellent analysis in *Comedy and Feminist Interpretation of the Hebrew Bible: A Subversive Collaboration* (Oxford: Oxford University Press, 2012), 116-42.

[3]Fun fact: the Hebrew in Judges is ambiguous enough that it can be read as though the angel is actually Samson's father. Some scholars speculate that Samson might be one of the Nephilim, the race of heroes created when the "sons of God" mated with the "daughters of humans" (Genesis 6:4). Goliath is also said to have been one of the Nephilim.

[4]In the epilogue of the book, Israel basically devolves into civil war. They had wandered so far from who God called them to be that they didn't need an outside nation to oppress them. God raised up no judge in the war, because no judge could save Israel from herself. Talk about bleak!

[5]Assuming our enemies are animalistic, uncultured, and less than fully human says a lot more about us than it does our enemies.

[6]For an in-depth analysis of current scholarship, see Eric Cline's excellent book *1177 B.C.: The Year Civilization Collapsed.*

[7]Three of those cities feature prominently in Samson's story: Ekron was closest to his home. He killed thirty Philistine lords of Ashkelon for the thirty garments he owed for losing the riddle wager at his wedding. He tore down the gates of Gaza after sleeping with a prostitute. The other two cities are Ashdod and Gath (hometown of Goliath).

[8]Judges 1:19 tells us, "Judah . . . could not drive out the inhabitants of the plain, because they had chariots of iron." Similarly, 1 Samuel 13:19-22 relates that the Philistines prevented the Israelites from building forges so they could not craft iron weapons.

[9]This was unthinkable in Israelite culture. The notable exception, Deborah (Judges 4), is still identified by her husband (wife of Lappidoth) and works in concert with a male general.

[10]For a fuller exploration of Genesis 1 as a cosmic temple text, see John H. Walton, *The Lost World of Genesis One* (Downers Grove, IL: IVP Academic, 2009).

[11]Though most English Bibles translate *torah* as "Law," a more faithful rendering of the word is "instruction" or "way." The *torah* is a path that leads to God, as Paul observes in Galatians 3:24.

[12]See Mary Douglas's landmark essay "The Forbidden Animals in Leviticus," *Journal for the Study of the Old Testament* 59 (1993): 3-23, for

insight into how the Torah extends the creation logic of Genesis 1 into the dietary code.

[13]In recent years, we've begun to modify many of these rules to allow for more liberty. So "don't dance" has become an injunction to avoid "all forms of dancing that detract from spiritual growth and break down proper moral inhibitions and reserve." See Dean G. Blevins, Charles D. Crow, David E. Downs, Paul W. Thornhill, and David P. Wilson, *Manual 2009–2013*, Church of the Nazarene (Kansas City, MO: Nazarene Publishing House, 2009), 50.

[14]See David Kinnaman and Gabe Lyons, *Unchristian* (Grand Rapids: Baker Books, 2007), for a challenging exploration of how American evangelicals are perceived by the larger culture.

[15]I explore this concept of contagious holiness more fully in JR. Forasteros, "A Contagious Holiness: Jesus, Dexter, and Walter White at the Super Bowl," in *Renovating Holiness*, ed. Josh Broward and Thomas Jay Oord (Nampa, ID: SacraSage Press, 2015), 109-14.

[16]There's nothing wrong with T-shirts and music. They just don't make us holy.

6 House of Cards

[1]We're seeing the rise of the corporate empire today. It's companies like McDonald's, Walmart, Google, and Apple that are colonizing the world, shaping practices, beliefs, and behaviors, and promising their ~~subjects~~ customers life if only we'll buy what they're selling.

[2]The church has a long tradition of this. John the Revelator referred to a woman teaching heresy in Thyatira as "that woman Jezebel, who calls herself a prophet." He warned she would be thrown onto a bed with "those who commit adultery with her" (see Revelation 2:18-28).

[3]Commandment 1 (Exodus 20:3) is nonnegotiable.

[4]To put that in perspective, Washington, DC, won't be two thousand years old until the year 3790.

[5]This was the same period the Philistines arrived on Israel's shore.

[6]Baal was a fertility god. He slept during the winter, which is why nothing grew, and so had to be awakened each spring in a fertility festival.

[7]Ahab's elder son, Ahaziah, ruled only two years. He died because he fell off a balcony. Ahab's family really should have avoided two-story structures.

[8]Thomas Hobbes, *Leviathan*, trans. Noel Malcolm, digital ed. (Chios Classics: n.p., 2012), location 1367.

[9]The irony is that they have no idea what they're asking for. Two rebels will be crucified at Jesus' right and left at his moment of glory.

[10]"No one has greater love than this, to lay down one's life for one's friends" (John 15:13).

[11]This is one reason the doctrine of the Trinity is so primary for the church. Because God exists as three in one, God can give and receive freely within the Godhead. God can be fully God—a giver—without anyone or anything else. God doesn't *need* us. God is free to create us out of love.

[12]You absolutely should read Neil Gaiman's contemporary fantasy classic *American Gods*.

[13]See M. Scott Peck, *The Different Drum: Community Making and Peace* (New York: Simon and Schuster, 1998), 86-105. I'm grateful to my friend Sue Sweeney for introducing me to Peck's overview of community. Sue is a curriculum and instruction specialist for a school district and is part of the preaching team at Catalyst, the church where I pastor.

[14]For a debate to be helpful and fruitful, both parties should be able to articulate their opponents' position as well as *or better than* the other can. Sit with that for a moment. Imagine your next debate if you adhered to this rule.

8 Between Rome and a Hard Place

[1]The film is based on the book of the same name by Dennis Lehane, a writer of hard-boiled, noir-ish detective novels and a staff writer on *The Wire*, one of the greatest TV shows of all time.

[2]Church tradition has assigned the fictitious three magi names. The cathedral in Cologne, Germany—which is the second largest in the world—even has the coffins of these three kings on display.

[3]Though we get our words *magic* and *magician* from *magi*, Zoroastrians didn't practice sorcery. Rather they viewed astrology the way we think of cutting-edge science today. The Greeks did use the word *magi* to refer to sorcerers and magicians, which is how the word came to mean what it does to us today.

[4]The Hasmonean dynasty was founded by the brother of Judas Maccabeus, who led the rebellion that freed Israel from foreign rule for the first time since the Babylonian Exile. The dynasty lasted about a century.

[5]When Aaron's sons offered unholy sacrifices, they were burned alive (Leviticus 10:1-2). When a man named Uzzah touched the ark of the covenant to keep it from falling, he was struck dead (2 Samuel 6:6-7).

[6]A Kabbalistic legend claims that the high priest wore bells or a rope tied to his ankle in case he died in the presence of God. There is no historical basis for this legend, but it captures the sense of danger associated with God's holiness.

[7]That enemy was backed by none other than Parthia, which hoped to exploit the Roman civil war to take Israel for its own. More on that in a bit.

[8]Antony became half of the first power couple, Antony and Cleopatra. A shame they didn't get a power couple name: Antopatra? Clantony?

[9]For instance, Herod used cutting-edge engineering technology to create a harbor. He built a port city and named it Caesarea Maritima, "Caesar by the Sea." On the hill overlooking the harbor, Herod built a temple and dedicated it to Augustus. All of this infuriated the Jews, so to placate them, Herod expanded Yahweh's temple in Jerusalem. By the time his massive renovation was finished, the Jewish temple was the envy of the ancient world.

[10]Gordon Franz, "The Slaughter of the Innocents: Historical Fact or Legendary Fiction?," *Biblical Archaeology*, December 8, 2009, www.biblearchaeology.org/post/2009/12/08/The-Slaughter-of-the-Innocents-Historical-Fact-or-Legendary-Fiction.aspx.

[11]Spencer Ackerman, "41 Men Targeted but 1,147 People Killed: US Drone Strikes—the Facts on the Ground," *The Guardian*, November 24, 2014, www.theguardian.com/us-news/2014/nov/24/-sp-us-drone-strikes-kill-1147. Micah Zenko, "Obama's Drone Warfare Legacy," *Politics, Power, and Preventive Action* (blog), January 12, 2016, www.cfr.org/blog/obamas-drone-warfare-legacy, shows that, as of 2016, US drones have killed 470 civilians, which accounts for more than 12 percent of total killed. The number is generally agreed to be very conservative, given the difficulty of obtaining accurate reports of casualty numbers.

[12]Derek Thompson, "The Myth That Americans Are Busier Than Ever," *Atlantic*, May 21, 2014, www.theatlantic.com/business/archive/2014/05/the-myth-that-americans-are-busier-than-ever/371350.

[13]Chris Isidore and Tami Luhby, "Turns Out Americans Work Really Hard . . . but Some Want to Work Harder," CNN Money, July 9, 2015, http://money.cnn.com/2015/07/09/news/economy/americans-work-bush.

[14]"Regular" attendance once implied weekly. Today it's more often two times per month at best. Further, a generation ago, many regular churchgoers attended three times weekly: Sunday morning, Sunday evening, and some sort of midweek gathering. Today many "regular" attenders participate only in the main weekend worship gathering.

[15]Shane Hipps, *Selling Water by the River: A Book About the Life Jesus Promised and the Religion That Gets in the Way* (New York: Jericho Books, 2012), 159.

10 The Cat's in the Cradle

[1]Mark 6:14-19. Note that Mark called Herod II "Philip." This is not Philip the Tetrarch (who Salome married), which has led scholars to wonder if Herod II was called Herod Philip. It's equally possible Mark had as much trouble sorting out Herodias's family tree as we do, and he didn't have the luxury of Wikipedia to consult. Don't blame Mark. Blame Herod.

[2]A few years after Jesus' death and resurrection, this conflict with Nabatea spilled over into all-out war. Antipas was deposed by Rome and exiled with Herodias to Gaul (modern-day France).

[3]Matthew and Luke, who used Mark as a source in writing their Gospels, diminished Herodias's role in John's death significantly. Matthew attributed her rage to Antipas, and she appeared in the story only after Salome's dance. Luke didn't mention her at all.

[4]Mariamne was the Hasmonean princess Herod married to secure his claim to the throne of Israel.

[5]That is probably the most confusing sentence in human history. Why do they all have to be named Herod?

[6]The Herodians weren't allowed to call themselves kings. Augustus gave them the title *tetrarch,* which meant "ruler of a quarter"—just in case they forgot who was in charge.

[7]In Jesus' day, Pontius Pilate served as the governor of Judea.

[8]While Augustus lived, Livia enjoyed the freedom to do as she pleased and became very popular among the Roman citizens. After Augustus's death, Livia faced increasing opposition from the Senate and her own son, Tiberius, because of her unwomanly pursuit of power.

[9]If that's not messed up enough, try this: then I would imagine that God decreed backward in time extra pain for Jesus to suffer on the cross each

time I did something wrong. My love of theology and science fiction combined to create a perfect shame engine.

[10]See M. Glasser, I. Kolvin, D. Campbell, A. Glasser, I. Leitch, and S. Farrelly, "Cycle of Child Sexual Abuse: Links Between Being a Victim and Becoming a Perpetrator," *British Journal of Psychiatry* 179 (2001): 482-94.

[11]Robert Barron, *And Now I See: A Theology of Transformation* (New York: Crossroad, 1998), 49.

[12]That trash bit is frankly terrifying. If you want to become very self-conscious about throwing away anything, read the excellent graphic novel *Trashed* by Derf Backderf.

[13]I am painfully aware this is not everyone's experience in church. I pastor a whole community of people who bear terrible scars they received at the hands of church people. We'll address this in the coming chapters.

12 What Death Smells Like

[1]Kerioth is the name of a city in the far southern reaches of Judea, about ten miles south of Hebron, where Herod the Great was buried. Kerioth was not far from Idumea, the birth country of Herod's father.

[2]Another idea, employed by Tosca Lee in her excellent book *Iscariot,* is that Judas was a member of the Sicarii, an assassins' organization dedicated to driving Rome out of Israel. This is obviously the most awesome option, but many scholars doubt the Sicarii were active in Jesus' day.

[3]Not everyone expected a messiah. The Sadducees, for instance, did not believe in a messiah at all.

[4]Most scholars agree that Mark was written first, and Matthew and Luke used Mark as a primary source material for their Gospels. About 85 percent of Mark's Gospel is reproduced in Matthew and Luke.

[5]Fun fact: a good translation of the Greek is "Follow me, Satan." So what's the antidote to a wrong picture of Jesus? Get behind him and start acting like him.

[6]Scholars call this the "Messianic Secret."

[7]Isaiah 66:1, for instance, describes heaven as God's throne and the earth as God's footstool. Psalm 132, a song pilgrims sang as they made their way toward Jerusalem, encourages travelers, "Let us go to his dwelling place; let us worship at his footstool" (v. 7).

[8]Luke moved the story to Jesus' Galilean ministry. In his version, Simon is a Pharisee who disrespects Jesus, while the woman is "a sinner." John

moved the story to the beginning of Holy Week, before the Triumphal Entry. Instead of Simon, Lazarus—who had just been raised from the dead—threw the banquet, and his sister Mary (of Mary and Martha) was the one who anointed Jesus.

[9]Because Luke and John remove this story from its place in Holy Week, they also ascribe motivations to Judas we don't find in Mark or Matthew. Luke tells us that Satan entered Judas, while John claims Judas was a crook who stole from the Twelve's common purse. Judas may have skimmed some money, and that's unquestionably wrong, but one sin does not imply or necessitate the other. Judas could have been a thief and not a betrayer.

[10]See Jesus' conversation with Nicodemus in John 3. Nicodemus struggled much as Judas did, but in the end, Nicodemus was at the foot of the cross, giving his king a royal burial.

[11]Mark Driscoll, in "7 Big Questions," *Relevant*, January/February 2007, http://web.archive.org/web/20071013102203/http://relevantmagazine.com/god_article.php?id=7418.

[12]What this pastor and many others reading Revelation 19 miss is that Jesus' robe is dipped in blood *before* the battle begins (v. 13). In Revelation, Jesus is the always-slaughtered Lamb, the God whose very nature is most perfectly revealed not as a ferocious, roaring lion, but as a lamb willingly offering himself up to death for us. He is not a warrior with "the commitment to make someone bleed," but a warrior whose sword is his very creative Word, whose only weapon is truth itself—a truth most fully expressed on the cross where he died.

[13]I have a cross tattoo, so that's not a dig on those who have them.

[14]Indeed, we have no easy analog in our culture for the shame the cross meant to the first-century world. As James Cone observed, the nearest may be the lynch mob's noose. See his *The Cross and the Lynching Tree*.

[15]Lecrae, Twitter post, July 4, 2016, 12:05 p.m., https://twitter.com/lecrae/status/750012773212401665/.

[16]Steve, Twitter post, July 4, 2016, 12:55 p.m., https://twitter.com/Hevi_On_Honkers/status/750025267117076480.

[17]See Peter Enns, *The Sin of Certainty* (New York: HarperCollins, 2016). He writes, "When we grab hold of 'correct' thinking for dear life, when we refuse to let go because we think that doing so means letting go of God, when we dig in our heels and stay firmly planted even when we sense that

we need to let go and move on, at that point we are trusting our thoughts rather than God. We have turned away from God's invitation to trust in order to cling to an idol. The need for certainty is sin because it works off of fear and limits God to our mental images. And God does not like being boxed in" (19).

[18]For a hilarious, provocative, and insightful exploration of this, read *My Imaginary Jesus* by Matt Mikalatos.

14 Running with the Devil

[1]My mother later suggested he simply wanted to spend time with me and was trying to get my attention. Right, Mom. *As if!*

[2]If we're making lists of artists we think might be satanic, let's start with Nickelback, Coldplay, and Justin Timberlake.

[3]See Origen, *Origen Against Celsus*, in *Fathers of the Third Century: Tertullian, Part Fourth; Minucius Felix; Commodian; Origen, Parts First and Second*, ed. A. C. Coxe, vol. 4 of *Ante-Nicene Fathers*, ed. Alexander Roberts and James Donaldson (Buffalo, NY: Christian Literature Company, 1885), 592.

[4]Origen's methodology is clear in his *Against Celsus*, chap. 44. He makes sweeping identifications of the devil because "every one who prefers vice and a vicious life is (because acting in a manner contrary to virtue) Satanas, that is, an 'adversary' to the Son of God" (p. 593). His allegorical reading of Scripture allows him to claim that historical persons are actually Satan, a hermeneutic that makes modern readers uncomfortable at best.

[5]In his commentary on Isaiah, Calvin wrote, "The exposition of this passage, which some have given, as if it referred to Satan, has arisen from ignorance; for the context plainly shows that these statements must be understood in reference to the king of the Babylonians. But when passages of Scripture are taken up at random, and no attention is paid to the context, we need not wonder that mistakes of this kind frequently arise. Yet it was an instance of very gross ignorance to imagine that Lucifer was the king of devils, and that the Prophet gave him this name. But as these inventions have no probability whatever, let us pass by them as useless fables." John Calvin, *Commentary on Isaiah*, vol. 1, trans. William Pringle (Grand Rapids: Christian Classic Ethereal Library, n.d.), www.ccel.org/ccel/calvin/calcom13.xxi.i.html.

[6]Fun fact: this is the passage used to claim Satan was the worship leader in heaven. In the King James Version, Ezekiel 28:13 reads, "The workmanship of thy tabrets and of thy pipes was prepared in thee in the day that thou wast created." Since tabrets and pipes are musical instruments, interpreters read them as metonymy, insisting that Satan was the first worship leader. Unfortunately for them (but fortunately for all of us who love rock 'n' roll!), the translation of those two Hebrew words is uncertain at best, and they probably don't refer to instruments at all. Whoops! Sorry, every hair metal band ever.

[7]Greg Boyd rightly observed that the "ancient serpent" John is referring to here is the Leviathan, a mythical sea serpent that embodied evil in the ancient Near Eastern imagination. See Gregory Boyd, *God at War: The Bible and Spiritual Conflict* (Downers Grove, IL: InterVarsity Press, 1997), 95.

[8]The book of Job, notably, refuses to do this. We'd do well to follow Job's lead and, at the end of our questions, throw up our hands and declare, "I have said too much already. / I have nothing more to say" (Job 40:5 NLT).

[9]See Shawna Dolansky, "How the Serpent Became Satan," *Biblical Archaeology*, April 8, 2016, www.biblicalarchaeology.org/daily/biblical-topics/bible-interpretation/how-the-serpent-became-satan. The idea of a talking snake is strange to us, but not to readers of this ancient text. Note too that neither the man nor the woman found the serpent's ability to speak unusual. Though the snake did test the man and woman, which we'll see is part of Satan's role, Genesis 3 doesn't identify the snake as anything other than a snake. It *could* be Satan, but nowhere in the whole of Scripture is this made explicit. Ancient readers would have known that snakes were considered symbols of wisdom in Babylonian culture. When read in light of the Babylonian exile, the story leaves no uncertainty as to how God feels about the wisdom of Babylon.

[10]John H. Walton calls this figure "The Challenger." See his discussion in Walton, *The NIV Application Commentary: Job* (Grand Rapids: Zondervan, 2012), 64.

[11]God tested the faithfulness of humanity throughout the Scriptures. God tested Abraham (Genesis 22:1) and Job. Moses saw the forty years in the wilderness as an extended time of testing (Deuteronomy 8:2). The Old Testament only talks in terms of *testing*, while in Greek, the same word is translated as both *tempting* and *testing*. To say that God tests us, then,

seems initially at odds with James's claim that God "tempts no one" (James 1:13). But James goes on to clarify that testing arises because of our sinful desires. In other words, if we weren't sinful, we'd ace the test. We experience temptations precisely because we are sinful.

[12]Satan is not alone in this. As in the book of Revelation, he marshals the powers of this world to deceive us. Government, media, education, economics, and even false teachers in the church herself assist in this mission of deception.

[13]See, for instance, Luke 7:33-34. He wasn't a drunkard or glutton, of course. But his opponents wouldn't have hurled such titles at him if he were more like his cousin John, a Nazirite who abstained from wine altogether. Jesus was apparently the life of the party—and why should that surprise anyone?

[14]Maybe it's not so surprising that the heaven this kind of religious person imagines is similarly dull. We often hear heaven described as flying around on clouds while playing harps. Boring! I bet they don't even allow any Ramones covers.

Epilogue: Empathy for the Devil

[1]As a fan of horror movies, it pains me to type that. Don't tell anyone I said it, okay?

[2]Julianna Baggott, "Author Julianna Baggott and the World of Pure," *The StoryMen*, Podcast audio, March 14, 2013, www.storymen.us/julianna-baggott.

Acknowledgments

[1]That's the *second* Grover reference (you know, from *Sesame Street*) in this book. You usually don't get one, and here I'm giving you two! Sure, it's in the acknowledgments, but it counts, right? It's a bonus treat for reading these.

CONTACT THE AUTHOR

Sign up for my mailing list to get updates on current projects, pop culture recommendations, and more! Go to jrforasteros .com/stuff.

I would love to connect with you. Find me on Facebook or Twitter (@jrforasteros). You can also send an email to jrforasteros@gmail.com.

I blog and podcast at NorvilleRogers.com. These are my podcasts:

- StoryMen—pop culture, history, and theology
- In All Things Charity—Wesleyan feminist theology (with two female pastors as cohosts)
- Don't Split Up!—reviews of horror films old and new
- Bible Bites—Sunday school for the twenty-first century (or Through the Bible Twenty Minutes at a Time)
- Origami Elephants—religion and philosophy through the lens of current events

You can also find my sermons at jrforasteros.com/messages.

You can download a discussion guide and sermon resources at empathyforthedevil.com.